GETTING THE MOST OUT OF YOUR
ELECTRONIC CALCULATOR

GETTING THE MOST OUT OF YOUR ELECTRONIC CALCULATOR

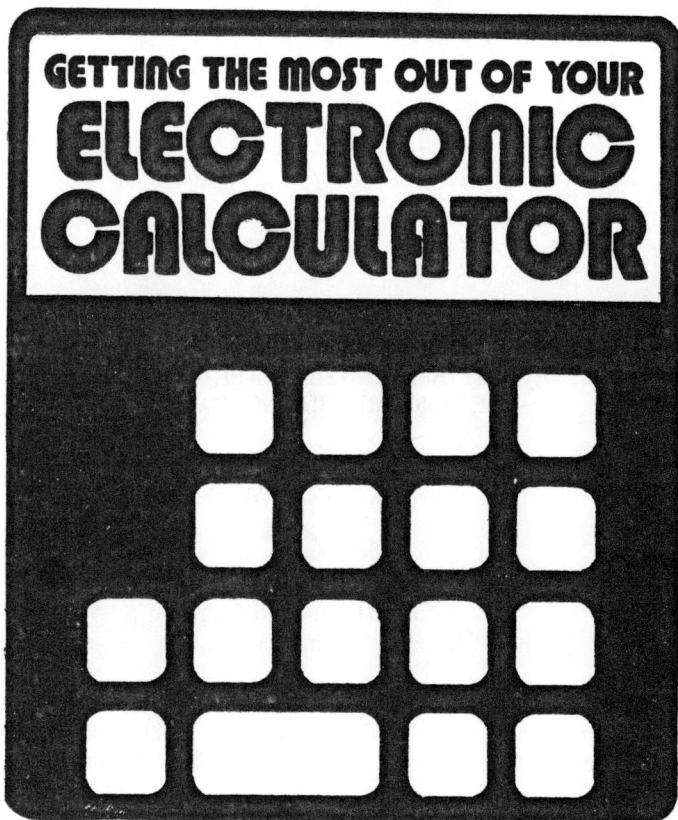

BY WILLIAM L. HUNTER

TAB BOOKS
Blue Ridge Summit, Pa. 17214

FIRST EDITION

FIRST PRINTING—APRIL 1974
SECOND PRINTING—OCTOBER 1974

Copyright ©1974 by TAB BOOKS

Printed in the United States
of America

Hardbound Edition: International Standard Book No. 0-8306-4724-4

Paperbound Edition: International Standard Book No. 0-8306-3724-9

Library of Congress Card Number: 74-5209

The electronic calculator is one of the most remarkable of all consumer products. It is a veritable electronic brain in a package often no larger than a pack of cigars.

Unfortunately, the little electronic brains—like most human brains—are usually operated at a mere fraction of their potential. One objective of this book is to enable the purchaser of a calculator to get the most out of his purchase. To that end, we present in this book numerous practical examples and shortcuts showing how to use the calculator for almost all everyday calculations, and how to get the right answer in the least time.

Another objective of this work is to serve as a modern course in general and commercial mathematics. As a math course, the book is modern—and, I believe, unique—in that it involves the use of a calculator instead of a pencil and paper. All of the problems found in traditional general math courses are here: square roots, ratios, averages, fractions, trigonometry, percentages, temperature and metric conversions, interest, etc.

If you are using this book in a math course, we hope that you will approach the course with enthusiasm, knowing that you are a prototype of the math student of the future. In studying math, your grandparents figured on a slate; your parents on a scratchpad. You are among the first to study math with the electronic calculator.

William L. Hunter

Contents

Features
and
Functions

The great scientific advances in electronics over the past few years have produced a remarkable instrument known as the electronic calculator. Basically, the data that is put into the instrument through the keyboard is electronically manipulated (by processes similar to those in giant data processing computers) to present an answer almost instantly on a display panel, or as a printout on a paper tape. Practically all of the electronic calculators manufactured today will accept a simple problem as it would commonly be written. For example, the problem, 25 x 25 =?, would be entered by depressing the appropriate keys in the same order in which the problem is written: 25 x 25 = 625. The answer would appear when the equal key was touched.

The basic keyboard for the input of numbers is the same as the keyboard on an adding machine. However, other keys are present that are not found on adding machines. All calculators will have a **multiply** key, a **divide** key, an **equal** key, a **clear** key, and others (such as a **clear entry** key), in addition to the usual **plus** and **minus** keys. The more advanced calculators have such function keys as square root, change of sign, pi, reciprocal, constant, trigonometric functions (sine, cosine, tangent), log base selector, log, inverse, and a wide variety of other functions. The various other functions are not exclusively mathematical. One manufacturer has programed two hundred years of calendars into a hand held calculator for use in interest and other day-associated calculations. The key used in these operations is simply marked "day." Some calculators have keys for one or two memory banks. Data that is computed by the calculating portion of the instrument can be stored in a separate part of the calculator, the memory, and recalled at will for further manipulation.

ADVANTAGE OF ELECTRONIC CALCULATORS

Anyone who has used both electronic and electromechanical calculators will probably say the most obvious advantage is speed. An electromechanical calculator may take several seconds to produce an aswer to a problem that an electronic calculator solves in thousandths of a second. This may not seem to be much of an advantage, but studies have shown that an accountant is far more efficient with the electronic calculator. Chain multiplication is accomplished almost as fast as figures can be entered, so complex problems are solved in seconds instead of minutes.

Simplicity of Operation

The very design of electronic calculators makes these instruments far superior to mechanical calculators. Although there are some very ingenious functions built into some mechanical calculators, electronic calculators are generally designed to almost instantly perform functions with one entry of figures, an example being the square root calculation. When a number is entered and the square root key depressed, the square root of that number is immediately displayed on the readout panel. No other entries or calculations are necessary. Complex problems involving multiplication and division are entered as the problem is observed, e.g., $(25/12) \times 3 \times 2.7 = 16.875$ would be entered in most electronic calculators exactly as shown, while intermediate steps are generally necessary in electromechanical calculators. Intermediate steps take time—time that is saved in using electronic calculators.

Quietness

Another very important consideration is noise. The conventional electromechanical calculator is about as noisy as an office typewriter when it is solving a problem, and solving a simple division problem can take several seconds. These mechanical calculators cannot be used where noise would be a problem, such as in a library or during a business conference. On the other hand, electronic calculators are practically silent in operation, except for printing calculators. When electronic calculators first came on the market, one manufacturer had to build a slight clicking sound into the keyboard to satisfy the operators. The operators were used to the click of the mechanical calculator, and needed the reassuring click to know the digits had been entered into the instrument.

There are several kinds of printing mechanisms in various makes of printing calculators (the discussion of which is beyond the scope of this book) and all produce some noise. Generally, the noise produced by the electronic printing calculator is not substantially less than the noise of an electric adding machine, although some instruments are much quieter than others. At least one manufacturer has developed a **thermal** printing electronic calculator, which is said to be

MELCOR MODEL 380—The manufacturer of the Melcor Model 380 has been in the electronics industry for over a decade. They have developed a shirt-pocket calculator with a memory and percent functions. The memory is not just a constant, but it is one that lets you perform individual extensions and accumulate results for a grand total and even more complex applications. And the memory isn't all that's new...they've added a percentage key that automatically performs percent calculations so you obtain decimally correct net percentage amounts in one easy step. The 380 has both fixed and floating decimal points, and is available with either the **Touch Tronic** pressure-sensitive keyboard, or the new "touch action" moving-button keyboard.

The unit accepts 8 digits of entry which it displays on its solid-state light-emitting readout. There is an indicator in the display to notify the operator of result overflow, and the calculator will not perform further until it is cleared to prevent errors. The automatic underflow system prevents errors where results are less than 0.0000001. An automatic **battery life extender** turns off the display 20-60 seconds after the last key operation to conserve battery life. The number on the display can be recalled by pressing the D key. Measuring just 5⅞ x 3 x ⅞ in., the unit weighs 5 ounces.

The unit's true algebraic memory stores negative or positive numbers. Single key operations perform entry, recall, and clear; and the memory can be used for storage, accumulation, or for a stored constant. The decimal point can be fixed up to 7 places, or it can operate in a floating point mode. **Melcor Electronics Corporation, 1750 New Highway, Farmingdale, New York 11735.**

almost silent in operation. The digits are printed on a special paper tape using a heat process.

Portability

Another advantage is size and portability. Relatively small mechanical calculators are produced that can be carried in a briefcase, but many kinds of battery-operated electronic calculators are small enough to be carried in a shirt pocket or purse. At least a dozen models weigh 8 oz or less, and one model weighs only 4 oz. Dimensions are as little as 2⅜ x ⅞ x 3½ in. One manufacturer makes a battery-operated electronic printing calculator that measures 4 x 8¼ x 1¼ in. and weighs about 1¾ lb. There is no doubt that further reductions in size and weight will be achieved as technology advances. Even with new lightweight materials available, mechanical calculators cannot compete in size and weight with electronic calculators.

Economy

An advantage that may outweigh all others to those with limited budgets is the price of electronic calculators. It is not possible to purchase a new mechanical or electromechanical calculator for $59.95, but several manufacturers of electronic calculators advertise this as the retail selling price of their product. The 4 oz unit mentioned above retails for about $100, and has a variety of functions.

The advantage of electronics has enabled manufacturers to include many features in electronic calculators that would be impractical in mechanical calculators. These features give electronic calculators a tremendous advantage over conventional calculators.

TYPES OF ELECTRONIC CALCULATORS

Although calculators have been classified into **personal** models and **office** models, there is no easy way to distinguish between the two. Because the small models are relatively inexpensive—even though considered to be personal models by the manufacturers—many small businesses find extensive use for these little electronic marvels. Conversely, the more expensive, multipurpose calculators are often found in home use, because the small minicalculators usually have only the four basic arithmetic functions (addition, subtraction, multiplication, and division), and the owners have determined that they need more features than just the basics.

Personal Calculators

More and more manufacturers are giving attention to the personal calculators, as the market is increasing in enormous proportions. Consumers are buying more and more calculators as the prices fall and the units become smaller and smaller. To reduce the prices means generally that the manufacturers must reduce the features. Therefore, personal calculators lack the capability of standard office models. Even so, there is nothing better for use in the field when quick, accurate analyses are necessary. Even the dependable slide rule is being set aside in favor of modern-day electronics.

Business and Scientific Units

Calculators can also be classified into **business** and **scientific** categories. Business calculators are generally of the office variety, and the functions found on these instruments pertain only to business mathematics. It is the purpose of this book to explain many of the problems that can be easily solved with business and personal calculators, rather than scientific problems. Scientific calculators will perform all the basic mathematical functions, but will also solve problems involving many types of technical data in just a single step. For example, sine of an angular value is found by simply entering the value and touching the **sin** key. Degrees, minutes, and seconds of arc converted to decimal equivalents by entering the angle and touching the appropriate key. Problems involving hyperbolic functions, trigonometry, exponents, degrees, radians, etc. are solved rapidly with scientific calculators.

Programmable Units

Other special-purpose calculators can be programed to perform complex calculations with great speed. One manufacturer declares that with his instrument over 4000 steps of programing, up to 522 complete arithmetic registers, symbolic logic, subroutines, and capability for up to 22 simultaneous equations fit into an area no bigger than the corner of a desktop. His computer is priced at around $3000, so it is not the type of electronic calculator that is found in the average home. It is beyond the scope of this book to discuss programmable calculators, other than to inform the reader that such devices do exist.

GENERAL PRICE RANGES

It has already been stated that several manufacturers offer electronic calculators for as little as $59.95 (manufacturer's suggested retail price). Some calculators are selling for as little as $39.95. In a recent survey, it was found that over 20 models were selling for $100 or less, and these models included a variety of features. Many portable pocket-size models are selling in this price range.

The moderately priced units, from $100 to $200, usually contain more functions and offer some features not available on lower priced models. The units selling for over $200 generally will accept more digits of entry, display more digits in the readout, contain more functions, and offer still more features than the moderately priced units. Although a few of the features found on the higher priced units are also found on some of the moderate and lower priced models, the higher priced instruments as a rule contain many more combinations of features and functions. For this reason, the reader should consider the primary functions he needs before he purchases an electronic calculator, and then purchase the model that best suits his needs.

The purchase of an electronic printing calculator requires considerably more of an investment than the ordinary display models, primarily due to the cost of the printing mechanism. Several models retail for less than $250, which is considerably less than what electromechanical calculators were selling for in the past decade. Prices on these models, depending upon the complexity of the electronics, range up to $7000. The obvious advantage to a printing calculator is that a printed record is made of each entry, while on the display models, each entry is displayed as entered, and the display is cleared automatically when the next entry is commenced.

FUNCTIONS AND KEYS

All electronic calculators perform the four basic functions—addition, subtraction, multiplication, and division. Some of the other functions briefly mentioned in prior paragraphs will be further detailed here by way of explanation of various key operations. The identifying symbols on the keys vary from machine to machine, but some of the more commonplace symbols are shown in parentheses in the discussion that follows.

Clear Key (C, C ALL, CLEAR, C A)

Different manufacturers identify this key in different ways, but the function is the same—it serves to clear the display, and in some cases the calculating registers. It is used prior to the initial entry of a problem to reset the instrument to zero. It is important to note that there is no industry standard to the assigning of identifying letters to certain keys. For example, C may not denote the clear key on one model while it does on the next. The key may clear the display only and eliminate a wrong entry in certain models, while not affecting the calculating registers at all. In other models, every register as well as the display is cleared. In small personal calculators, this key is usually identified as C, and it clears both the display and the registers. It is suggested that the instruction manual provided by the manufacturer with each calculator be consulted to determine the exact function of the clear keys.

Clear Entry Key (CE, C, CK, CL DIS, CLEAR DISPLAY)

This key may also be identified by different letters, depending upon the manufacturer and the model. The purpose of the key is to clear an erroneous keyboard entry. On display models, the erroneous entry will appear on the display, but will disappear when the clear entry key is depressed, while on printing calculators, the function is to simply remove the entry from the internal register and reset the register to zero. The operation of this key in most models will have no effect on the portion of the problem previously entered. Although the letters CE are the identifying letters most commonly found in smaller calculators for this function, it is suggested that the instruction manual be consulted to determine the exact description of the clear entry key. Not all models of personal calculators are provided with this key, so before buying an instrument, determine if a need for this function exists and if the key is available on the model under consideration.

Add Key (+)

After a number has been entered into the keyboard, depressing this key adds the number to the operating register. In display models, the number entered and previous entries will be algebraically totaled and displayed, while in printing calculators, the figure entered will simply be printed on the paper tape. Not all electronic calculators have an add key—in a relatively few models the equal key performs the same function.

Minus Key (—)

After a number has been entered in the keyboard, depressing this key subtracts the number entered from the amount in the operating register. If the answer is negative, most calculators will indicate that the display is a negative figure. The display operates as described above—the algebraic total of the figures entered in the operating register are displayed. In printing calculators, the number entered will be printed on the paper tape, along with an identifying symbol to indicate a negative entry.

Multiply Key (×)

This key is depressed after the first factor—the multiplicand—of a multiplication problem has been entered in the keyboard. Operation of this key sets up the instrument for subsequent multiplication. On display models, the multiplicand appears on the display as the figures are entered on the keyboard, while in the printing calculator, the input is printed on the tape along with an identifying symbol only when the multiply key is depressed.

Divide Key (÷)

This key is depressed after the first factor of a division problem—the dividend—has been entered in the keyboard. Operation of this key sets up the input for subsequent division. On display models, the dividend appears on the display as the figures are entered on the keyboard, while in the printing calculator, the input is printed on the tape along with an identifying symbol only when the divide key is depressed.

Equal Key (=)

When this key is depressed, the actual calculations are initiated within the instrument, and the answer displayed on the display panel. In the printing calculator, the results are internally coupled to the printer, and then printed on the tape. The equal key may also be used to obtain a total when printing calculators are used. On display models, when the problem involves only addition and subtraction, the answer is calculated and displayed as the problem is entered—so the equal key is not used.

The problem 2 + 3 + 4, for example, is entered as if the calculator is an adding machine. When the first digit, 2, is entered in the keyboard, it will appear automatically on the display, and when the + key is depressed to instruct the machine to add this figure to the following figures (and to any figure already in the operating register), the instrument will hold this figure in the operating register and await further instructions. When the next digit, 3, is entered on the keyboard, a 3 will appear on the display, and when the + key is depressed, the sum of 2 and 3—or 5—will appear on the display. The next digit, 4, will appear (and 5 will disappear) when it is entered in the keyboard. Again, the sum of 4 and 5— or 9— will appear on the display when the + key is depressed. Therefore, it is not necessary to use the equal key. As previously stated, in some models the equal function and the plus function are combined on one key.

Decimal Point Key (.)

In electronic calculators—as opposed to elec- tromechanical calculators—it is possible to insert the decimal point when the problem involving a decimal is entered into the keyboard, using the decimal point key. At the conclusion of the calculation, the answer appears with the decimal point in its proper place. The capability of operating in this way is often referred to as **floating decimal.** Before the advent of the electronic calculator, the location of the decimal point had to be separately determined (with few exceptions), which took time and also allowed the possibility of error. The method of setting the decimal to the desired number of places in the electronic calculator varies with different models, although most use a floating decimal. In some models, the decimal is set by use of a rotary switch.

Total Key (T, TOTAL, TOT)

As a general rule, the total key is not found on display models, since the total is carried forward on the display as the problem is entered in the keyboard and the plus or minus key depressed. On printing calculators, the key is used to print the total on the tape.

Constant Key (K)

The constant key does not physically operate in the same manner as the number keys; that is, it is usually a locking switch mechanism. On some models, the key will remain locked in after it has been depressed, and will return to its normal state, or off, only after being depressed again. On other models, the constant key is in fact a toggle switch. Activating this function will cause certain figures to be stored in a special memory for use in multiplication and division problems, which is convenient if the same figure is to be used successively in multiplication or division. If a series of numbers are to be multiplied by 8, for example, then 8 is a constant. It is entered only once for the entire series, in the constant memory. With the constant switch activated, the first entry of a multiplication problem may be used as a constant. In a division problem, the second entry may be used as a constant divisor. (This is not the case with all models, and many models have no constant key at all.) The constant function will be explored further in later chapters on practical applications of the electronic calculator.

The more expensive calculators have a wide range of functions, many for specialized operations. It is recommended that the instruction manual associated with each instrument be consulted for further details.

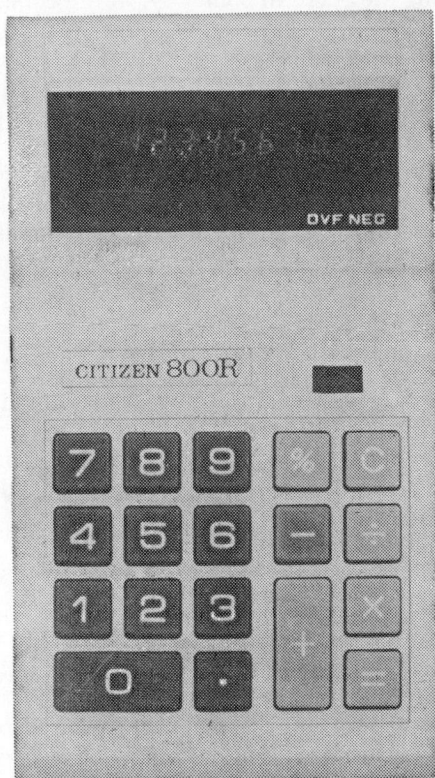

CIMATRON MODEL 800R—The Cimatron Citizen Model 800R is an ac-dc electronic calculator designed for maximum ease of operation with little or no eyestrain for the user. It has a large 8-digit display, and yet measures only 1¼ x 3¼ x 6 inches, and it weighs just 9½ ounces. The display is of the Digitron type, and the logic circuitry is single chip MOS-LSI. The decimal system is the floating/fixed type, and the large keyboard allows for man-size operation.

The 800R features a live percent key, and an add key with repeat addition, adding percentages, and doubling. The clear (C) key has dual functions—it will clear the last entry when pressed once, leaving the previous entry and command, and will clear all entries when pressed twice. When the display is in overflow, pressing the clear key will remove the overflow flag and leave the result on the display for further calculation. Any number can be repeatedly added or subtracted without reentry by repeatedly pressing the plus or minus keys, as the case may be. To double any number, the plus key is simply pressed twice.

The unit features chain multiplication and division, constant (when a certain number is to be used consecutively for multiplication or division), and true credit balance. **Cimatron Company, 1710 22nd Street, Santa Monica, California 90404.**

QUALITY AND PERFORMANCE

It has been several years since electronic calculators were first mass-produced for the consumer market, but during that period of time, many consumer complaints were registered against the manufacturers. Many bugs were found in production models that were not evident when the instrument was purchased, but appeared later when the calculator was put into daily use.

Many reputable office machine dealers refused to sell electronic calculators because of the poor quality and frequency of repairs. Up until recently, electronic printing calculators were placed in this category, even though the design defects had been worked out of the display models.

With the advent of the electronic calculator and the potential sales that were possible in the huge American marketplace, many companies entered the field. The rush was on to produce a product as quickly as possible, and in the rush, quality was sometimes overlooked. It is interesting that practically none of the manufacturers of electromechanical calculators offered electronic calculators during the early years. It was not that these manufacturers lacked interest— just the opposite was true. The fact was that the old reliable companies had a reputation to maintain, and at the risk of losing sales, remained out of the market until they were convinced they had produced a quality product that would perform over the years as advertised.

The display calculator was the first type to achieve acceptance as a reliable instrument. It has no moving parts, except for those used by the operator, and uses basic electronic principles well proven over the years. Gradually, the electronic printing calculator was perfected, and it is now found in thousands of businesses around the world.

Competition has proven to be a major factor in bringing about quality and performance in electronic calculators. Most of the models of today—whether display or printing—are of very good quality, and should provide years of trouble-free service.

SERVICING CONSIDERATIONS

It may be difficult to find a dealer to service some of the unknown, imported electronic calculators. The office machine dealer who is expert at repairing electromechanical machines may fall flat on his face in solving electronic problems. Most of these dealers return a defective unit to the distributor or to the manufacturer for repair, as they are not equipped or trained in repairing electronic equipment. To merely set up to repair electronic calculators requires a considerable investment in instrumentation, which many dealers are unwilling or unable to make. As a result, it usually takes longer for service on electronic calculators than it does for conventional calculators.

A few manufacturers have designed **plug-in modules** to facilitate rapid repair. Instruments with this feature are understandably more expensive, since plugs and sockets must be wired into the unit. A dealer who stocks parts for these units may be able to repair them quickly.

In larger cities, certain companies specialize in repairing electronic instrumentation, and oftentimes dealers who are not equipped to perform repair service will obtain the assistance of these specialists for maintenance. Sometimes, manufacturers will seek out these repair companies and contract with them to be "official" repair stations.

Factory repair service is most always available—even if local service is not—so a unit can eventually be repaired. It may be advisable to determine how service is to be performed when a unit is purchased, but the fact that service is not as readily available on electronic calculators as on electromechanical calculators should not deter the purchase of any model.

LACK OF STANDARDS

There are no standards in the manufacture of electronic calculators, and many instruments have features that others do not have. Calculators that have floating decimals do not require the presetting of decimal places, but since presetting is required on many models, the procedure for solving the examples in this chapter include this step. It is recommended that the instruction manual supplied with each calculator by the manufacturer be reviewed to determine its various features.

Basic Mathematics

2

Broken down into parts, mathematics is simple. Long equations used by engineers and scientists are easily performed on electronic calculators designed for scientific applications. But when personal calculators with limited functions are used, certain problems may take a little longer to solve. The secret is to break each problem down into parts.

This chapter deals with the basic mathematical functions of addition, subtraction, multiplication, and division. The problem is presented, and the step-by-step entries that are to be made into the electronic calculator are explained, so that similar problems may be easily solved. The primary purpose of this chapter is to assist the user in becoming thoroughly familiar with the calculator and its uses. Many practical problems in simple mathematics are presented, along with the procedures to be followed in solving these problems. In some cases, a problem may be solved using several different methods, but in each problem herein, the solution provided is the approach consistent with the four basic functions of the personal calculator. It is often possible to solve the problems in this and the following chapters in fewer steps if certain additional functions are available on the calculator used. As the user becomes more familiar with his instrument, he may wish to deviate from the procedures given, depending upon the capabilities of his calculator.

Throughout the text, the example problems and procedures for solving them assume that a display calculator will be used by the reader. Since there is no "standard" electronic calculator, the procedures necessary to solve a given problem on the user's instrument may vary slightly from the procedures stated in this book. The solutions are just as applicable to the electronic printing calculator, but the printout on paper tape is not identical with the electronic display. By following the procedures given, the same answer will always be obtained, no matter which electronic calculator is used.

The problems in this chapter deal with basic mathematical functions—addition, subtraction, multiplication, division, and extracting roots. It is essential that these operations be thoroughly understood.

SIMPLE ADDITION

To perform addition on the electronic calculator, first enter on the keyboard the number to be added, and then touch the plus key. As the number is entered on the keyboard, it will be displayed on the display panel, making it easy to check for errors. When the plus key is depressed, the number entered will be placed in the add register, where it is held awaiting the next entry. In most models, the last number entered will remain on the display until the function key is touched. In an addition problem the total amount stored in the add register will be displayed after the add key is actuated. For example, if we enter the number 35 on the keyboard, that number will be displayed. After we touch the plus key, 35 will continue to be displayed if the add registers were cleared before the number was entered. Suppose we want to add 10 to this number. The display will be a 1 (clearing 35 from the display) as soon as the 1 is entered on the keyboard. When the 0 is entered on the keyboard, 10 will be displayed, but as soon as the plus key is touched, the display will be 45. The 45 is a **running total,** and the figure stored in the add register.

Numbers that are to be added are called **addends,** and the answer is referred to as the **sum** (or total). Simple addition of two numbers is easily performed on the calculator.

Simple Addition

Perform the following addition:

$$23 + 78 = ?$$

Procedure

Operation	Keyboard Entry	Function Touch	Display	Description
Set decimal to 0				
Clear registers and display		C	0	
Enter first addend	23	+	23	
Enter second addend	78	+	101	Sum

In this problem, the first step is to set the decimal to 0. Many models of calculators do not have a mechanical method of setting the decimal, since it is set automatically by the calculator electronics. Throughout this book, we have included the instruction of setting the decimal, but this is to be disregarded if a floating decimal feature is available on the calculator in use.

The above problem might be written out 23 + 78 = ?. Note that we did not enter the problem into the calculator exactly as it is written here. It was not necessary for us to use the equal key, as the running total in the add register was shown on the display.

Few problems are presented to us as mere sets of numbers. Most are associated with data of some kind. In mathematics books, these are called **word problems**. Many word problems are included in this book.

Word Problem

Diane and Lynda were selling tickets to the school play. Diane sold 87 tickets and Lynda sold 88. How many tickets did the two girls sell?

Procedure

Operation	Keyboard Entry	Function Touch	Display	Description
Set decimal to 0				
Clear registers and display		C	0	
Enter number of tickets that Diane sold	87	+	87	
Enter number of tickets that Lynda sold	88	+	175	Answer

Normally, the calculator finds extensive household use as an adding machine, whether it is rechecking the cash register tape from the grocery store, checking the bank's figures on the bank statement, or working on that annual nightmare—the income tax return.

Adding a List of Figures

To become familiar with adding a list of figures, perform the following exercise:

$$
\begin{array}{r}
273 \\
261 \\
27 \\
8 \\
+ \ 1216 \\
\end{array}
$$

Procedure

Operation	Keyboard Entry	Function Touch	Display	Description
Set decimal to 0				
Clear registers and display		C	0	
Enter first addend	273	+	273	
Enter second addend	261	+	534	Sum of first two addends
Enter third addend	27	+	561	Sum of first three addends
Enter fourth addend	8	+	569	Sum of first four addends
Enter fifth addend	1216	+	1785	Answer

In this problem, a comma separating the hundreds from thousands can be written by the operator when the answer is transferred from the display to paper, as 1,785.

SIMPLE SUBTRACTION

Two different methods of entering subtraction problems are currently being used by electronic calculator manufacturers. One method is to enter the problem exactly as it is written. For example, $22 - 11 = ?$ can be solved by entering 22 on the keyboard, depressing the minus function key, entering 11, and depressing the equal key. The answer will then appear on the display. The other method, which is followed in this book, is to enter the problem exactly as it would be entered in a mechanical adding machine. The above problem is solved by entering 22 on the keyboard, depressing the plus function key, entering 11, and depressing the minus key. The answer will then appear on the display, without the necessity of depressing the equal function key. Remember that in this book the latter method is used; it will be necessary to make the appropriate adjustments when the problem is entered. The instruction manual supplied with the instrument will contain the method used in that model.

In subtraction problems, the first number is called the **minuend,** and the second the **subtrahend.** The answer is the **remainder.**

Subtraction on the Calculator

Perform the following subtraction:

$$
\begin{array}{r}
2275 \\
-811 \\
\hline
?
\end{array}
$$

Procedure

Operation	Keyboard Entry	Function Touch	Display	Description
Set decimal to 0				
Clear registers and display		C	0	
Enter minuend	2275	+	2275	
Enter subtrahend	811	−	1464	Remainder

The answer is 1464.

Money Problem

The following word problem deals with money. With most calculators it is necessary to enter a decimal point when money is involved, unless we are using only whole dollars in our calculations. When entering dollars and cents (or only cents, as in this problem), we merely touch the decimal point key between the dollars and cents (or before entering the cents if only cents are involved). Solve the following word problem:

Dan went to the store with $0.55 to buy some candy. When he returned, he had $0.29 left. How much did he spend for candy?

Procedure

Operation	Keyboard Entry	Function Touch	Display	Description
Set decimal to 2 places				
Clear registers and display		C	0	
Enter minuend (decimal point first)	.55	+	.55	
Enter subtrahend	.29	−	.26	Answer

SIMPLE MULTIPLICATION

Multiplication is performed almost instantly on the electronic calculator. The multiplication problem is made up of the **multiplicand** and the **multiplier.** The answer is called the **product** of the two. Multiplication problems are entered exactly as they are written. For example, 2 x 3 =? would be solved by entering 2 on the keyboard, depressing the multiply function key, entering 3, and then depressing the equal function key.

Multiplying on the Calculator

Perform the following multiplication:

$$281 \times 56 = ?$$

Procedure

Operation	Keyboard Entry	Function Touch	Display	Description
Set decimal to 0				
Clear registers and display		C	0	
Enter multiplicand	281	x	281	
Enter multiplier	56	=	15736	Product

The answer is 15,736.

Installment Payments

Installment payments are commonplace in our society, and it is sometimes necessary to determine the total amount of the installment payments. The following word problem involves simple multiplication:

Marc bought an automobile and agreed to pay $83 a month for 36 months. What is the total amount of the payments?

Procedure

Operation	Keyboard Entry	Function Touch	Display	Description
Set decimal to 0				
Clear registers and display		C	0	
Enter payment amount	83	x	83	
Enter number of months	36	=	2988	Answer

Marc will have paid $2988 in payments when the automobile is paid for.

SIMPLE DIVISION

Division is the reverse of multiplication. The number to be divided is the **dividend**, while the number by which we divide is the **divisor**. The answer is called the **quotient**. Division problems are entered exactly as they are written. As an example, $6 / 3 = ?$ would be solved by entering 6 on the keyboard, depressing the divide function key, entering 3, and then depressing the equal function key.

Division on the Calculator

Solve the following division problem:

$$20720 / 37 = ?$$

SUMMIT MODEL K08M—The K08M is a miniature one-chip calculator with a built-in memory, with memory storage and retrieval accomplished with a single key. The compact size of the unit makes one-hand operation of the memory and all other functions simple and convenient. Featuring true algebraic logic, the unit will accept direct negative entries without locking up the keyboard. In addition to the memory system, the instrument has a single key, automatic percentage figuring and allows additions and subtractions from original figures with reentry. Answers are always decimal correct with the K08M, since it contains a full floating decimal system, but it also has a decimal selection from 0 to 7, set by the decimal key. Numbers are automatically rounded off in all preset positions, and unwanted zeros are suppressed.

The calculator has an 8-digit entry and readout, with a 16-digit calculating capacity. It performs both mixed and chain calculations, and gives true credit balance answers. An automatic overflow protection system prevents wrong answers as a result of digit overrun.

The unit weighs 8¼ ounces and measures only 2¾ x 4 x 1⅛ inches. It is fully functional on ac or dc, with built-in nickel-cadmium batteries that provide 10 hours of continuous use. The batteries can be recharged in only 3 hours. Each unit is delivered with an ac-dc adapter / charter and deluxe padded carrying pouch. **Summit International Corporation, 180 West 2950 South, Salt Lake City, Utah 84115.**

Procedure

Operation	Keyboard Entry	Function Touch	Display	Description
Set decimal to 0				
Clear registers and display		C	0	
Enter dividend	20720	÷	20720	
Enter divisor	37	=	560	Quotient

It might be advisable to set the decimal to two or three places before starting a division problem, to determine if a remainder exists. If a remainder exists a number other than zero will appear to the right of the decimal point. In calculators that have the floating decimal feature, the decimal point will be placed automatically in the answer if a remainder exists.

Finding Unit Cost

A wholesaler sold 81 bicycles to a dealer for $4212. How much did each bicycle cost the dealer?

Procedure

Operation	Keyboard Entry	Function Touch	Display	Description
Set decimal to 0				
Clear registers and display		C	0	
Enter total cost of bicycles	4212	÷	4212	
Enter number of bicycles	81	=	52	Answer

The bicycles cost the dealer $52 each.

ADDING WITH DECIMALS

Adding figures with decimals is much simpler with the electronic calculator than with the familiar adding machine. Numbers such as 3.001, 6.9, 8.28, and 16 can be added on the adding machine, but zeros must be entered after each number, except for the first one, so that three decimal places exist in each number. The number 6.9 would be entered as 6.900, 8.28 as 8.280, etc. Zeros do not need to be added with the electronic calculator.

Decimal Addition

Add 3.001, 6.9, 8.28 and 16.

Procedure

Operation	Keyboard Entry	Function Touch	Display	Description
Set decimal to three places				
Clear registers and display		C	0.000	
Enter first number (be sure to enter decimal point)	3.001	+	3.001	
Enter second number	6.9	+	9.901	
Enter third number	8.28	+	18.181	
Enter fourth number	16	+	34.181	Answer

The calculator will automatically position the decimal point in its proper place. It is not necessary to enter zeros after any numbers, as long as the decimal point is entered correctly.

SUBTRACTING WITH DECIMALS

Subtraction problems involving decimals are performed in the same manner as addition problems, except that the minus function is used rather than the addition function. (See previous problem.)

Decimal Subtraction

Solve the following problem:

$$3.001 - 6.9 = ?$$

Procedure

Operation	Keyboard Entry	Function Touch	Display	Description
Set decimal to three places				
Clear registers and display		C	0.000	
Enter first number	3.001	+	3.001	
Enter second number	6.9	−	−3.899	Answer

Note that the answer is a negative number. Most electronic calculators will indicate negative answers by the use of an indicator light.

COMBINATION ADDITION AND SUBTRACTION CALCULATIONS

A problem containing both addition and subtraction factors is easily performed on the calculator. As we mentioned

UNICOM MODEL 201—Unicom Systems is a division of Rockwell International, one of the largest corporations in the United States. They have produced the Unicom Model 201, which has a number of desirable features. Individual calculations can be tucked away in a memory for grand totals which are instantly recalled by the push of a button. Figures need not be reentered each time. With automatic constants, you can multiply or divide by the same number, over and over again, without having to reenter that number. A live percent key allows any percentage calculation—discounts, taxes, commissions, markups, whatever—to be figured automatically.

A large, easy-to-read display is bright but still easy on the eyes. Green numbers flash on an 8-digit display that is two times larger than that of most other minis. A flip of the switch gives you a choice of fully floating or floating-in / fixed out of 2 places. And the 201 lets you work mixed calculations in a continuous flow, without having to obtain intermediate answers. The instrument uses 4 inexpensive penlight batteries for over 10 hours of continuous operation. An optional ac-dc charger kit is also available.

The unit is 6 x 3¼ x 1½ inches, and weighs 12 ounces. **Unicom Systems, Rockwell International, 10670 N. Tantau Avenue, Cupertino, California 95014.**

earlier, there are two different methods of handling subtraction problems, depending on the model of calculator being used. This book uses the method in which the minus sign is entered after the number has been entered on the keyboard. To perform addition and subtraction with a series of numbers, enter each number on the keyboard, and depress the appropriate add or subtract function key. For example, in the problem $2 + 3 - 4 + 5 - 6 = ?$, enter 2, depress the plus function key, enter 3, depress the plus function key, enter 4, depress the minus function key, enter 5, depress the plus function key, enter 6, and depress the minus function key. The answer will appear on the display.

Addition and Subtraction

Solve the following addition and subtraction combination problem:

$$20 + 66.24 - 27.6 + 14.007 - 33 + 8.08 + 2 = ?$$

Procedure

Operation	Keyboard Entry	Function Touch	Display	Description
Set decimal to three places				
Clear registers and display		C	0.000	
Enter first number	20	+	20.000	
Enter second number	66.24	+	86.240	
Enter third number	27.6	−	58.640	
Enter fourth number	14.007	+	72.647	
Enter fifth number	33	−	39.647	
Enter sixth number	8.08	+	47.727	
Enter seventh number	2	+	49.727	Answer

MULTIPLYING DECIMAL NUMBERS

The important thing to remember when multiplying figures containing decimals is to be sure and enter the decimal point where it belongs in the problem. All electronic calculators have a decimal point on the keyboard, and will electronically place the decimal point at its proper location in the answer. If the calculator being used does not have a floating decimal, it will be necessary to set the decimal before beginning the problem. This book assumes that the decimal point must be set, and therefore provides an instruction for setting the decimal point. However, this instruction may be ignored if the decimal floats, because the calculator electronics will automatically place the decimal point correctly in the display.

Multiplying figures containing decimals is not different than multiplying figures without decimals. The difference is that if there is a decimal point in the number being entered, the decimal point must be entered also.

Multiplication with Decimals

Solve the following problem:

$$\$2.79 \times 6.93 = ?$$

There is a total of four decimal places in this problem, so in order to obtain an exact answer, the decimal switch must be set to four places. However, if an exact answer is not required, the setting may be less than four. For example, if a person earned $2.79 per hour, and worked 6.93 hours, how much would be earned? Carrying out the answer to ten-thousandths of a dollar is unnecessary, since a dollar can only be divided into hundredths.

Procedure

Operation	Keyboard Entry	Function Touch	Display	Description
Set decimal to four places				
Clear registers and display		C	0.000	
Enter first number	2.79	x	2.7900	
Enter second number	6.93	=	19.3347	Answer

Most of the personal calculators do not round off. If wages were to be determined in the above problem, it would be necessary to set the decimal to at least three places, and the operator would have to mentally do the rounding. The display would be 19.334, and rounded off, the wages would be $19.33.

DIVIDING DECIMAL NUMBERS

Figures containing decimals for division are entered in the same manner as any other figure that contains a decimal. The operation is carried out as for a normal division problem without a decimal. The operator must make sure that the decimal point is entered correctly when the number is entered on the keyboard. The decimal point will then be correctly placed automatically in the answer by the calculator electronics.

Combined Multiplication and Division

Solve the following problem, which entails both multiplication and division operations:

Dan earns $156.71 a week, if he works 40 hours. Last week he worked only 38.6 hours. How much did he earn?

This problem has two parts. The first is to determine how much per hour Dan earns, and the second is to multiply his hourly wage times the number of hours worked.

Procedure

Operation	Keyboard Entry	Function Touch	Display	Description
Set decimal to four places				
Clear registers and display		C	0.0000	
Enter normal weekly wages	156.71	÷	156.7100	
Divide by 40 hours	40	x	3.91775	Wages earned per hour
Multiply by hours worked	38.6	=	151.2251	Earnings

Notice that in this two-step operation the equal sign was not used until the end of the problem. When the multiply function key was touched, the calculator performed the operation it had been set up to do previously, and that was to divide 156.71 by 40. The quotient was set up as a multiplicand when the multiply function key was touched, and upon entry of the multiplier, 38.6, the instrument was ready to perform its final calculation in the problem when the equal key was touched. The wages earned in this problem would be rounded to $151.22. The third and fourth decimal places (which disappear upon rounding) are called **guard figures**. Two guard figures are found to be adequate for almost any problem that is done on a calculator. Very extended problems require three or more guard figures, while one guard figure suffices for simple problems.

ADDING FIGURES BEYOND THE CAPACITY OF THE CALCULATOR

Practically all of the small personal electronic calculators are limited to eight-digit input capacity. However, it is possible to add numbers with unlimited digits, as shown in the following problem.

Adding Large Numbers

$5,171,238.25$
$+2,313,901.11$

The problem must be broken down into simple parts that can be handled by the calculator:

$$\begin{array}{cc} 5171 \\ 2313 \end{array} \text{ Set 1} \qquad \begin{array}{cc} 238.25 \\ 901.11 \end{array} \text{ Set 2}$$

Procedure

Operation	Keyboard Entry	Function Touch	Display	Description
Set decimal to two places				
Clear registers and display		C	0.00	
Enter first addend from set 2	238.25	+	238.25	
Enter second addend from set 2	901.11	+	1139.36	Last five digits of display are last five digits of answer; first digit is carry-over.

At this point the problem is only half-solved. Note that there are six digits on the display. The last five digits are the last five digits of the final answer. Since the calculator will be cleared in the next sequence, these digits must be recorded separately. The first digit of the display is carried over into the next step as follows:

Procedure

Operation	Keyboard Entry	Function Touch	Display	Description
Clear registers and display		C	0.00	
Set decimal to 0				
Enter first digit of previous calculation	1	+	1	
Enter first addend from set 1	5171	+	5172	
Enter second addend from set 1	2313	+	7485	First four digits of final answer

We now combine the first four digits of the final answer, 7485, with the last five digits, 139.36, and by placing the dollar sign and commas in the correct place, arrive at an answer of $7,485,139.36.

34

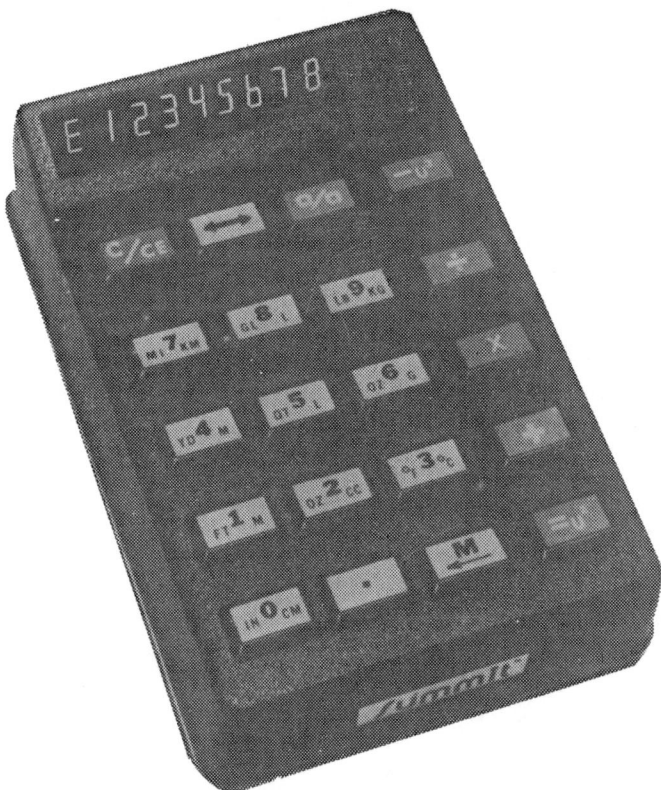

SUMMIT MODEL MCC—One of the most interesting of the small personal electronic calculators is Summit's Model MCC, a **U.S. to metric conversion** computer that doubles as a 5-function calculator with a memory. U.S. measurements are easily converted to metric terms, or metric to U.S. To change from U.S. to metric terms, first enter the number, then press the "convert" key. The subscript programs are now waiting for your selection. Press the key with the subscript program you want, such as yards to meters, and the computer electronically converts the number of yards to the correct meter measurement. To change metric measurements to U.S. terms, press the "reverse" key after the "convert" key. The U2 and U3 subscripts are entered when you are working with square and cubic measurements.

As a miniature calculator, the MCC will add, subtract, multiply, divide, directly figure percentages, and store and retrieve numbers in its memory. It weighs only 8¼ ounces and measures just 2¾ x 4 x 1⅜ inches. In a short 3 hours, its ac charger will recharge the built-in ni-cad batteries to give 10 hours of operating time.

The conversion units found on the keyboard are **gallons to liters, miles to kilometers, quarts to liters, yards to meters, feet to meters, ounces to cubic centimeters, inches to centimeters, pounds to kilograms, ounces to grams,** and **Fahrenheit to Celsius (centigrade).**

A completely American product, the instrument comes with a deluxe padded carrying pouch and an ac charger. **Summit International Corporation, 180 West 2950 South, Salt Lake City, Utah 84115.**

SQUARE ROOTS

The square root of a given number is the number that, multiplied by itself yields the given number as the product of the multiplication. The cube root of a given number is the number that taken as a factor three times in self-multiplication yields the given number as the product.

Although many electronic calculators have the automatic square root feature, the inexpensive models generally do not. On units that do have the feature, the procedure is simple. The operator merely enters on the keyboard the number, and then depresses the square root key, which is generally marked with the letters SQ RT or with the square root symbol ($\sqrt{}$). The answer appears on the display panel. Some models do not have a square root key, but do have the feature built into the unit. On these instruments, the number whose square root is desired is entered on the keyboard, and in sequential order, the divide key and the equal key are depressed. The square root then appears on the display panel.

Electronic calculators that have only the four basic functions (add, subtract, multiply, and divide) can be used to determine square roots. The method used is based on an approximation derived by Sir Isaac Newton. Initially, a good guess is made at the approximate square root, and Newton's formula is applied using the guess. The result of the calculations using Newton's formula will be closer to the correct answer than the original estimate, but still will not be correct. This result becomes the second guess, and Newton's formula is applied again. When successive estimates tend to be the same, the square root has been obtained. After each application of Newton's formula, the result of the calculations can be multiplied by itself to determine if a sufficiently close answer has been produced.

Newton's formula states that the square of the guess (estimate) plus the number whose root is sought will produce a sum that, when divided by twice the guess, will result in a new estimate that is closer to the square root than the first guess:

$$\frac{\text{Square of guess plus number whose root is sought}}{\text{Twice the guess}} = \frac{\text{New}}{\text{estimate}}$$

For example, assume that the square root of the number 1234 is desired. As our first guess, we know that 30 x 30 = 900, while 40 x 40 = 1600; so our first guess must be somewhere between 30 and 40. If 35 is chosen as the first guess, the problem appears as follows:

36

$$\frac{(35 \times 35) + 1234}{2 \times 35} = \text{New estimate}$$

The number 35 will be replaced by the new estimate, and the same operation performed to obtain the next estimate, which will be still closer to the correct answer. Any number may be used as a first guess, but the closer the guess is to the actual square root, the fewer will be the number of calculations required.

The following problems explain how Newton's formula can be applied to any situation where the square root of a number is desired. The number whose square root is to be found is called the **radicand.**

Calculation of Square Root of a Number

Determine the square root of the number 1089, within an accuracy of two decimal places.

Since square root calculations involve extended calculations, it will be necessary to carry at least two guard figures (a guard figure is a number found in a decimal place in excess of the number of decimal places required in the answer). Our intermediate calculations should be carried to four decimal places—two places required in the answer and two guard places. Since 30 x 30 = 900, and 40 x 40 = 1600, we know that the answer lies somewhere between 30 and 40. As a first guess, we will choose 35.

Procedure

Operation	Keyboard Entry	Function Touch		Description
Set decimal to four places				
Clear registers and display		C	0.0000	
Enter first guess	35	x	35.0000	First guess
Reenter first guess	35	=	1225.0000	Square of first guess
Transfer display to add register	None	+	1225.0000	
Add radicand (number whose square root is to be determined)	1089	+	2314.0000	Square of first guess plus number whose root is sought
Transfer display to divide register	None	÷	2314.0000	
Enter 2	2	÷	1157.0000	
Reenter first guess	35	=	33.0571	

At this point, we must start a new cycle, with the new estimate just obtained as our second estimate.

Procedure

Operation	Keyboard Entry	Function Touch	Display	Description
Transfer display to multiply register	None	x	33.0571	Second estimate
Enter second estimate	33.0571	=	1092.7718	Square of second estimate
Transfer display to add register	None	+	1092.7718	
Add radicand	1089	+	2181.7718	Square of second estimate plus number whose root is sought
Transfer display to divide register	None	÷	2181.7718	
Enter 2	2	÷	1090.8859	
Reenter second estimate	33.0571	=	33.0000	New estimate (third guess)
Transfer display to multiply register	None	x	33.0000	(Start of third cycle)
Enter third estimate	33.0000	=	1089.0000	Radicand

Calculations are terminated at this time, since we have obtained the original radicand by squaring the third estimate (33.0000). By rounding off the guard figures, the number 33.00 has been determined to be the square root of 1089.

Since a reasonably good guess was made and used as the first estimate, the answer to the problem was obtained in only two cycles. Using this method, each succeeding answer will be closer to the actual square root (35.0000, 33.0571, 33.0000), and if a mistake is made somewhere in the calculations, Newton's method will self-correct, immediately zeroing in on the correct answer again.

If the instrument in use will not transfer the display to the add, divide, and multiply registers; simply record the display, clear it, reenter the display figures in the keyboard, and depress the appropriate function key (add, divide, or multiply).

Square Root Word Problem Using Newton's Method

Farmer Jack has a square one-acre parcel of land at the intersection of Northsouth Highway and Eastwest Road. Big Sahara Oil Co. has offered him $100 per frontage foot for this parcel. Littlehorn Refiners, Inc. has offered him a flat $60,000 for the parcel. Which offer should he take? There are 640 acres to the square mile and there are 5280 ft to the mile. Farmer

Jack must determine how many frontage feet he has on each of the two roads in order to compare the two offers.

Procedure

Operation	Keyboard Entry	Function Touch	Display	Description
Set decimal to 0				
Clear registers and display		C	0	
Enter feet in a mile	5280	x	5280	
Reenter feet in a mile	5280	=	27878400	Square feet in a square mile
Transfer display to divide register	None	÷	27878400	
Enter acres in a square mile	640	=	43560	Square feet in an acre (record)
Clear registers and display		C	0	
Set decimal to two places				
Enter first guess of square root of 43,560	200	x	200.00	First guess
Reenter first guess	200	=	40000.00	Square of first guess
Transfer display to add register	None	+	40000.00	
Add radicand	43560	=	83560.00	Square of first guess plus number whose root is sought
Transfer display to divide register	None	÷	83560.00	
Enter 2	2	÷	41780.00	
Reenter first guess	200	=	208.90	New estimate (record)
Transfer display to multiply register	None	x	208.90	Second estimate (begin new cycle)
Reenter second estimate	208.90	=	43639.21	Square of second estimate
Transfer display to add register	None	+	43639.21	
Add radicand	43560	=	87199.21	Square of second estimate plus number whose root is sought
Transfer display to divide register	None	÷	87199.21	
Enter 2	2	÷	43599.60	
Reenter second estimate	208.90	=	208.71	New estimate (third estimate)

Since there is very little change between the second estimate and the last estimate, we will conclude that the last figure is sufficient for our purposes. This figure represents the feet along one side (frontage) of the square one acre plot. This figure must be doubled to determine the frontage on the two roads.

Procedure

Operation	Keyboard Entry	Function Touch	Display	Description
Transfer display to multiply register	None	x	208.71	
Enter 2	2	=	417.42	Farmer Jack's frontage feet on 2 roads
Transfer display to multiply register	None	x	417.42	
Enter $100 per frontage foot	100	=	41742.00	Big Sahara's dollar offer

Since $60,000 is offered by Littlehorn as against only $41,742 by Big Sahara, Farmer Jack should take Littlehorn's offer.

CUBE ROOTS

The **cube root** of a given number is a number that, when taken as a factor three times in self-multiplication, yields the given number as the product of these multiplications. The **cube** of a given number, on the other hand, is the product of the number multiplied by itself and the result of that calculation multiplied again by the given number. For example:

$$\sqrt[3]{64} = 4; \ = .4^3 = 4 \times 4 \times 4 = 64$$

Few, if any, of the lower priced electronic calculators have the automatic square root function, not to mention the automatic cube root function. However, there is another formula based on Newton's approximation, for determining the cube root of a number. As with the square root formula (see preceding problems), a good guess is made—this time as to the approximate cube root—and then Newton's cube root formula applied using the guess, or estimate. The result of the calculations using Newton's formula will be closer to the correct answer than the estimate, but probably still will not be correct. The result is the second guess, and Newton's formula is applied again. When successive results tend to be the same, the cube root has been obtained.

Newton's cube root formula states that twice the cube of the guess (estimate), plus the number whose cube root is sought, will produce a sum which, divided by three times the square of the guess, yields a new estimate that is a closer approximation to the cube root.

$$\frac{2 \times (\text{guess})^3 + \text{number whose cube root is sought}}{3 \times (\text{guess})^2} = \text{New estimate}$$

For example, assume that the cube root of the number 2345 is desired. For our first guess, we reason that 10 x 10 x 10= 1000, while 15 x 15 x 15 = 3375; so our first estimate must be somewhere between 10 and 15. If 13 is chosen as the first guess, the problem will appear as follows:

$$\frac{(2 \times 13 \times 13 \times 13) + 2345}{3 \times 13 \times 13} = \text{New estimate}$$

In the second application (or cycle) of Newton's formula, the number 13 will be replaced by the new estimate, since this number is closer to the correct answer. Any number may be used as a first guess, but the closer the guess is to the actual cube root, the fewer will be the number of calculations required. The number whose cube root is to be found is called the **radicand** (as in the square root problems).

Cube Root Using Newton's Method

Find the cube root of 65, within an accuracy of two decimal places.

Since the cube root calculations are extended ones, it will be necessary to carry at least two guard figures. Since 4 x 4 x 4 = 64, we know the answer lies near 4; so, as our first guess, we will choose 4.

Procedure

Operation	Keyboard Entry	Function Touch	Display	Description
Set decimal to four places				
Clear registers and display		C	0.0000	
Enter 2	2	x	2.0000	
Enter first guess	4	x	8.0000	
Reenter first guess	4	x	32.0000	
Reenter first guess	4		128.0000	Twice the cube of the first guess
Transfer display to add register	None	+	128.0000	
Enter radicand	65	=	193.0000	
Transfer display to divide register	None	÷	193.0000	
Enter 3	3	÷	64.3333	
Enter4	4	÷	16.0833	
Enter 4	4	=	4.0208	Second estimate (record)

Instead of multiplying 3 x 4 x 4 to obtain the divisor in Newton's formula (three times the square of the guess), mathematical principles will allow us to simply divide those figures sequentially as was done above, and the quotient will be the same, the next estimate in the series. We are now ready to begin the next cycle.

Procedure

Operation	Keyboard Entry	Function Touch	Display	Description
Transfer display to multiply register	None	x	4.0208	
Reenter second estimate	4.0208	x	16.1668	
Reenter second estimate	4.0208	x	65.0034	Cube of second estimate (almost equals given number)
Enter 2	2	=	130.0068	Twice the cube of the second estimate
Transfer display to add register	None	+	130.0068	
Enter radicand	65	=	195.0068	
Transfer display to divide register	None	÷	195.0068	
Enter 3	3	÷	65.0022	
Enter 4.0208 (second estimate)	4.0208	÷	16.1664	
Reenter 4.0208	4.0208	=	4.0206	Third estimate

The difference between the second estimate and the third estimate is only 0.0002, and since we have to be accurate within only two decimal places, we may accept this last answer as the final answer. By rounding, we obtain 4.02 as the cube root of 65.

Homework

3

A number of problems found in high school mathematics courses are included in this chapter. It is not wise for the student to use the calculator in solving his homework problems, since he is unable to use a calculator during his classes or his examinations, and since he will learn far less if he uses the calculator. However, his answers can be readily checked with the instrument. The problems here are usually of a practical nature and can frequently be applied to everyday situations. It is recommended that the reader carefully review this chapter so that he may relate these problems to problems that confront him from time to time in his ordinary activities.

The exercises in this chapter will further help familiarize the operator with the capabilities of the electronic calculator.

WORD PROBLEMS

Most of the problems in this chapter are word problems. Any problem involving ordinary addition, subtraction, multiplication, or division where the problem is spelled out in detail, such as $25 \div 3 = ?$, can be solved by merely entering the numbers and depressing the proper function keys. The hardest part of Junior's homework is generally understanding how to express the problem in terms that can be entered on the keyboard. This chapter begins with relatively easy problems, and progresses to the more difficult. A wide range of word problems is presented.

COMMON MATHEMATICAL PROBLEMS

In the previous chapter we explored many simple operations that are performed on the electronic calculator. In this chapter, we will explore some more difficult problems common to high school mathematics. The topics include addition, subtraction, multiplication, division, elementary algebra, value comparison, averages, mixed calculations (problems involving combinations of addition, subtraction, multiplication, and division), angles, percentages, profit calculations, percentage comparisons, price markup and markdown, sale price calculations, commissions, fractions,

BOWMAR MODEL MX70—The **Bowmar Brains** are America's top selling personal calculators, according to the manufacturer. The MX70 is a full-function rechargeable hand-held electronic calculator with memory bank and omni-constant. The unit features a memory storage and recall system, extra large LED 8-digit display, and a full floating decimal system. The omni-constant is Bowmar's description of an automatic constant with a brain.

Using the memory recall function, it is possible to transfer to the display any number stored in the memory system. This number may then be used in any further calculation. The MX70 has a minus sign, overflow, low-battery, and memory indicators, and with the ni-cad battery, it will provide 5 hours of continuous operating time. It requires 7 hours to fully recharge the batteries with the charger accessory.

The unit is guaranteed one year, and measures 5 x 3 x 1½ inches. It weighs 8 ounces. **Bowmar Consumer Products Division, 531 Main Street, Acton, Mass. 01720.**

decimals, time distribution, piecework calculations, and others. The problem is presented, and then the step-by-step operations necessary to solve the problem are given. In many instances, we must rearrange the problem so that it may be entered in the calculator. These methods are typical in solving similar types of problems.

ADDITION, SUBTRACTION, MULTIPLICATION, AND DIVISION

A series of problems of the basic functions of the calculator are included in this section. While these problems are not very difficult, they will help to establish a firm understanding of the calculator. The first problem involves addition of a series of numbers.

Addition

A department store chain has 837 stores in the East, 533 stores in the South, 1049 stores in the Midwest, and 482 stores in the West. What is the total number of stores in the chain?

Procedure

Operation	Keyboard Entry	Function Touch	Display	Description
Set decimal to 0				
Clear registers and display		C	0	
Enter first addend	837	+	837	
Enter second addend	533	+	1370	
Enter third addend	1049	+	2419	
Enter last addend	482	+	2901	Answer

The answer is that there are 2901 stores in the chain.

After the last entry, it would be possible to touch the equal key and obtain the same results. In fact, some calculators combine the plus key with the equal key. Usually, on these same models, the minus key is combined with an equal key, too. These two dual-function keys allow the manufacturer to eliminate a separate equal key.

The following problem is a six-digit subtraction problem. It is rapidly solved on the electronic calculator.

Subtraction

The ABC Flea Market needed to expand, and was looking over two different parcels of land to purchase for its new building. One parcel of land had an area of 287,629 sq ft (square feet), and the other an area of 303,466 sq ft. How many square feet larger was the second parcel than the first?

Procedure

Operation	Keyboard Entry	Function Touch	Display	Description
Set decimal to 0				
Clear registers and display		C	0	
Enter area of larger parcel	303466	+	303466	
Enter area of smaller parcel	287629	−	15837	Answer

The second parcel was 15,837 sq ft larger than the first parcel.

The next problem is a relatively easy multiplication problem:

Multiplication

A school has 43 classrooms, and each classroom has 35 chairs. What is the total number of chairs in the school's classrooms?

Procedure

Operation	Keyboard Entry	Function Touch	Display	Description
Set decimal to 0				
Clear registers and display		C	0	
Enter number of classrooms	43	x	43	
Enter number of chairs per classroom	35	=	1505	Answer

There is a total of 1505 chairs in all the classrooms.

The following division problem is a typical problem found in inventory control. As items are used, the inventory control manager must reorder to keep well stocked in anticipation of future requirements.

Division

A factory has 74,442 setnuts in inventory. If 114 setnuts are required for each cafipump manufactured, how many cafipumps can be made before the inventory is depleted?

Procedure

Operation	Keyboard Entry	Function Touch	Display	Description
Set decimal to 0				
Clear registers and display		C	0	
Enter number of setnuts in inventory	74442	÷	74442	
Enter number of setnuts needed for each cafipump	114	=	⟍653	Answer

MIXED CALCULATIONS

The problems that follow all use more than one of the four basic mathematical operations. The following cabfare calculation entails addition, subtraction, and multiplication.

Cabfare Calculation

If the cabfare is $0.70 for the first third of a mile, and $0.60 for each mile thereafter, what would the fare be for a trip of 11.3 miles?

Procedure

Operation	Keyboard Entry	Function Touch	Display	Description
Set decimal to three places				
Clear registers and display		C	0.000	
Enter total miles of trip	11.3	+	11.300	
Subtract first third of mile	.333	—	10.967	Miles at $0.60 per mile
Transfer display to multiply register	None	x	10.967	
Enter fare per mile	.60	=	6.580	Fare for all but first third of a mile
Transfer display to add register	None	+	6.580	
Enter fare for first third of a mile	.70	+	7.280	Answer (before rounding)

Rounded off, the fare would be $7.28.

Combination Multiplication and Subtraction

Shelby Insurance Co. pays $103 per week for janitorial services and maintenance. Smythe Funeral Homes pays $452 a month for the same type of services. Which firm pays more per year for these services, and how much more?

This problem involves two multiplication operations and a subtraction operation.

Procedure

Operation	Keyboard Entry	Function Touch	Display	Description
Set decimal to zero places				
Clear registers and display		C	0	
Enter Shelby's weekly payment	103	x	103	
Enter number of weeks in a year	52		5356	Shelby pays $5356 per year (record this figure)
Clear registers and display		C	0	
Enter Smythe's monthly payment	452	x	452	
Enter number of months in a year	12		5424	Smythe pays $5424 per year
Transfer last product to add register	None	+	5424	
Enter Shelby's annual payments (from prior calculation above)	5356	—	68	Answer to second part of problem

Smythe pays $68 per year more than Shelby for janitorial and maintenance services.

Tile-Setting Labor Cost

Dan charged $25 for setting tile on a wall 8 ft by 5.5 ft. Each tile occupied 1 sq in. How much did Dan charge for setting each tile? Round your answer to the nearest tenth of a cent.

This problem is solved by first finding how many square inches are involved on a wall 8 ft by 5.5 ft. (Each square foot contains 144 sq in.) The total number of square inches is then divided into $25.

Procedure

Operation	Keyboard Entry	Function Touch	Display	Description
Set decimal to four places				
Clear registers and display		C	0.0000	

Operation	Keyboard Entry	Function Touch	Display	Description
Enter wall height (multiplicand)	8	x	8.0000	
Enter wall width (multiplier)	5.5	x	44.0000	Square feet on wall
Enter number of square inches in sq ft	144	=	6336.0000	Square inches on wall (record answer)
Clear registers and display		C	0.0000	
Enter amount of earnings	25	÷	25.0000	
Enter square inches on wall	6336	=	.0039	Answer (before rounding)

Dan charged $0.0039 for setting each tile. Rounded to the nearest tenth of a cent, his charges were 0.4 cent per tile.

Finance Charge Calculation

Mr. Rogers was considering the purchase of an automobile. The price of the automobile was $2195. He was allowed $500 on his trade-in, and he financed the balance at 79.10 per month for 24 months, which included the finance charge. How much was the finance charge?

Procedure

Operation	Keyboard Entry	Function Touch	Display	Description
Set decimal to two places				
Clear registers and display		C	0.00	
Enter monthly payment	79.10	x	79.10	
Multiply by number of months payments are to be made	24	=	1898.40	Total amount of payments on amount financed (record answer)
Clear registers and display		C	0.00	
Enter price of automobile	2195.00	+	2195.00	
Subtract trade-in allowance	500.00	—	1695.00	Amount financed (record answer)
Clear registers and display		C	0.00	
Enter total amount of payments (from above)	1898.40	+	1898.40	
Enter amount financed (from above)	1695.00	—	203.40	Answer

SINGER FRIDEN MODEL 1008—Maximum calculating power, tiny dimensions, and complete portability are combined in the 1008 mini calculator. This little calculator, which weighs just over a pound, is not a lightweight at adding, subtracting, multiplying and dividing at electronic speeds through its miniature LSI circuits. Though only 5 x 7 inches in size, the 1008 has big-calculator features, including an 8-digit fluorescent tube display, positive and negative multiplication, true credit balance, constant factor multiplication and division, and power calculations.

An underflow answer protection feature signals the operator whenever the unit's capacity is exceeded. The most significant first 8 digits of the calculation are protected by shifting excess digits of the display to the right, with the decimal point indicating the number of digits eliminated. The keyboard is locked to protect further entries. A rechargeable, self-contained battery gives cordless power, making the unit equally useful for everything from business trips to shopping at the neighborhood supermarket. For ordinary use, the device plugs into standard power outlets.

The $325 price of the 1008 includes a travel cover and a powerpack adapter. The adapter keeps batteries charged even when the unit is being used with an ac power cord. It shuts off automatically when the battery is fully charged. A light on the display signals when the battery needs recharging. **Singer Business Machines Division, San Leandro, California 94577** ·

Many small calculators have functions that allow a shorter number of calculations to arrive at the answer. However, the procedure just described will provide the correct answer with all units now manufactured.

Cash Discount

The Adams Hardware Store ordered 3 doz Jamits at $1.79 each, 2 doz Whatizs at $2.61 each, and 7 doz Dozits at $0.26 each. The store received a 2-percent discount for paying the distributor within 10 days. How much did Adams have to pay for the merchandise?

Procedure

Operation	Keyboard Entry	Function Touch	Display	Description
Set decimal to two places				
Clear registers and display		C	0.00	
Enter cost of each Jamit	1.79	x	1.79	
Enter number of Jamits purchased (3 x 12)	36	=	64.44	Cost of Jamits before 2-percent discount (record answer)
Clear registers and display		C	0.00	
Enter cost of each Whatizs	2.61	x	2.61	
Enter number of Whatizs purchased (2 x 12)	24	=	62.64	Cost of Whatizs before 2-percent discount (record answer)
Clear registers and display		C	0.00	
Enter cost of each Dozit	.26	x	0.26	
Enter number of Dozits purchased (7 x 12)	84	+	21.84	Cost of Dozits before 2-percent discount
Enter total cost of Jamits from above calculation	64.44	+	86.28	
Enter total cost of Whatizs from above calculation	62.64	+	148.92	Total cost of all merchandise before 2-percent discount (record answer)
Set decimal to four places				
Clear registers and display		C	0.0000	
Enter total cost of all merchandise before discount	148.92	x	148.9200	
Enter discount of 2 percent	.02	=	2.9784	2-percent discount (record answer)

Operation	Keyboard Entry	Function Touch	Display	Description
Set decimal to two places		C		
Clear registers and display		+	0.00	
Enter total cost of all merchandise before discount	148.92	—	148.92	
Enter 2 percent discount (rounded off)	2.98	=	145.94	Answer

After entering the number of Dozits purchased (84), the plus key was operated, and the display was the product of $0.26, the cost of each Dozit, and the number of Dozits purchased. It might seem that the equal key should have been operated, but most of the personal calculators will perform the function just entered, regardless of what function key is operated. In this case, the multiply key was operated after the cost of each Dozit was entered, and after the number of Dozits purchased was entered, the operation of the plus key instructed the calculator to carry out the previous instruction (multiply), and to transfer the result to the add register. To obtain the total cost of the merchandise purchased prior to the discount, it was necessary only to add the cost of the Jamits and the Whatizs to the add register.

The discount of 2 percent must be entered in its decimal form. Since there were a total of four decimal places in the multiplier and the multiplicand, it became necessary to set the decimal switch to four places to permit proper rounding off.

AVERAGES AND COMPARISONS

To obtain an average, it is usually necessary to total all the component parts, and divide the total by another factor that is in some way related to the component parts. Finding averages is a frequent application of division, and division problems are handled exceedingly easily on the electronic calculator. If three books contain 56, 52, and 64 pages, respectively, we can determine the average number of pages in each book by adding all pages together, and then dividing by the number of books $(56 + 52 + 64 = 172, 172 \div 3 = 57.3)$.

A comparison is merely the measuring of one value or set of values against another value or set of values. The answer may be expressed in various terms—percentages, for example—or it may be stated simply as one value being larger than another.

Average Number of Students per Teacher

School boards are always determining the average number of students per teacher. The following is an example of such a determination.

If there are 99,766 students in the University of California, and 7,964 teachers, what is the average number of students per teacher? Carry your answer out to two decimal places.

Procedure

Operation	Keyboard Entry	Function Touch	Display	Description
Set decimal to three places				
Clear registers and display		C	0.000	
Enter number of students	99766	÷	99766.000	
Enter number of teachers	7964	=	12.527	Answer (before rounding)

There is an average of 12.53 students per teacher at the University of California.

Average Speed Calculation

Fireball rode his bicycle 298 miles without stopping in 24 hours. Find his average speed to the nearest tenth of a mile per hour.

Procedure

Operation	Keyboard Entry	Function Touch	Display	Description
Set decimal to two places				
Clear registers and display		C	0.00	
Enter total miles	298	÷	298.00	
Enter total hours	24	=	12.41	Answer (before rounding off)

When rounding off 12.41 to the nearest tenth, the answer becomes 12.4. Fireball averaged 12.4 mph on his 298-mile journey.

Population Comparison

Marketing managers of the nation's largest companies are always comparing marketing areas. Political organizations need to know the relative size of one area of the country as opposed to another. Advertising agencies must compare the cost of advertising in one population center as opposed to another. This problem compares the size of a small town in Nebraska with a large city in Massachusetts.

If Boston, Massachusetts, has a population of 641,071, and Wahoo, Nebraska, has a population of 3,835, how many times larger than Wahoo is Boston? Carry your answer out to one decimal place. The decimal must be set to two places to permit rounding off.

Procedure

Operation	Keyboard Entry	Function Touch	Display	Description
Set decimal to two places				
Clear registers and display		C	0.00	
Enter population of Boston	641071		641071.00	
Enter population of Wahoo	3835		167.16	Answer (before rounding)

Boston is 167.2 times larger than Wahoo.

ANGLES

Geometry students are continually required to calculate angles from a known set of values. Terms such as **acute, bisector, central, complementary, inscribed, obtuse,** etc. are very familiar to these students. Most of the effort in solving the following problem is in putting the problem in terms the calculator can handle.

If two angles total 90 degrees, they are said to be **complementary.** Assume that one complementary angle is 24 degrees larger than the other. Find the two angles. Let θ represent one angle. Then, the other angle must be ($\theta + 24$) degrees. Together, they must total 90 degrees; that is,

$$\theta + (\theta + 24) = 90$$

Combining

$$2\theta + 24 = 90$$

Transposing

$$2\theta = 90 - 24$$

Therefore

$$2\theta = 66, \text{ or } \theta = \frac{66}{2}$$

Procedure

Operation	Keyboard Entry	Function Touch	Display	Description
Set decimal to 0				
Clear registers and display		C	0	
Enter dividend	66	÷	66	
Enter divisor	2	=	33	Answer

Angle θ equals 33 degrees and angle (θ + 24) equals 57 degrees. To check the answer, add 33 and 57, and note that the sum is 90.

Note that many of these operations can be performed on the electronic calculator. Since these basic calculations have been previously explained, they are not given here.

PERCENTAGE

We are exposed to percentage calculations practically every day, in one way or another. Sales taxes are always calculated in percentage; interest rates are based on percentages; discounts are usually figured in percentages. Many other transactions use percentage calculations. Remember that **percent** is another way of saying **hundredths**, and hundredths can be expressed as a fraction or a decimal as well as in the percentage form. For example, $1/100$ equals 0.01 equals 1 percent. When percentage is used, it means the same as hundredths, so to change percentage to a decimal requires that we drop the percent sign and move the decimal point two places to the left. Conversely, changing from a decimal to percentage, we move the decimal point two places to the right and add the percent sign. On the electronic calculator, we multiply the display by 100 to change to percentage, and divide by 100 to change to a decimal equivalent. For example, 14 percent equals 0.14, 0.35 equals 35 percent, 12.3 percent equals 0.123, and 2.3456 equals 234.56 percent.

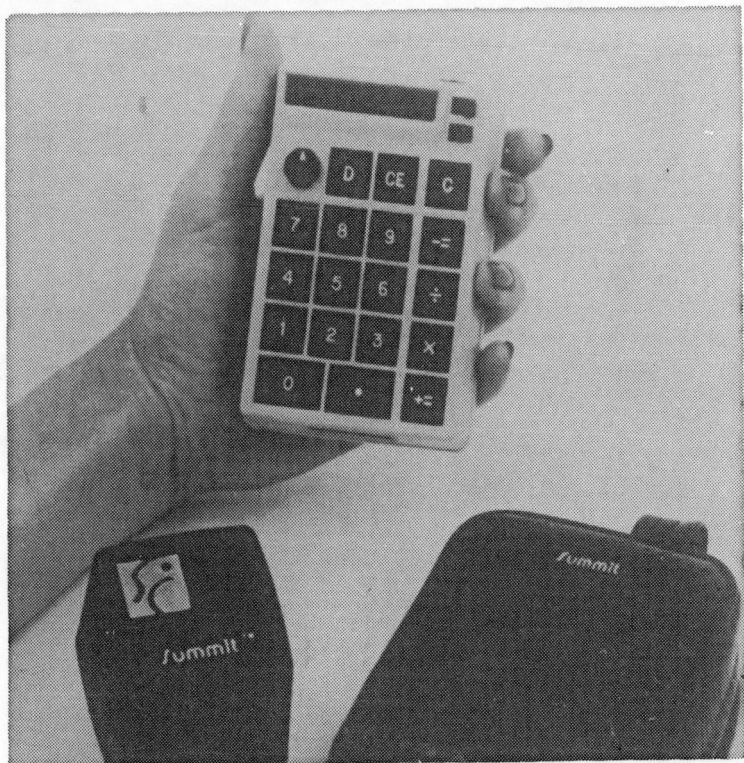

SUMMIT MODEL K08—The little Summit K08 miniature calculator is a shirt-pocket unit weighing only 8.2 ounces and measuring a petite 2¾ x 4 x 1⅛ inches. Its small size permits efficient one-hand operation. It is fully American made and represents the industry's most advanced technology in design and operation. It is backed by a one-year warranty of over-the-counter exchange.

The unit features 8-digit entry and readout, but it has 16-digit calculating capacity and automatic zero suppression. Special sign indicators signal entry errors, negative answers for true credit balance, and overflow. The decimal can be set for full floating, or to any place from 0 to 6, and the large, easy-to-use keyboard has finger contoured keys with a locator dot on the "5" key. Automatic entry overflow protection locks keyboard to prevent wrong answers. A **sign change** key permits change of a plus entry to a minus entry and vice versa, while algebraic logic permits multiplying a negative number by a positive number with the correct sign in the answer. The four basic functions can be used in mixed and chain calculations.

The K08 is housed in an attractive, break-resistant case designed to fit comfortably into the hand, and is fully functional on ac or its built-in nicad batteries. The unit will operate for 10 hours on dc, and will recharge in just 3 hours. (Indicator signals when batteries need recharging.) The instrument comes complete with an ac-dc charger and a deluxe padded pouch. **Summit International Corporation, 180 West 2950 South, Salt Lake City, Utah 84115.**

Percentage Calculation
What is 12.7 percent of 5280?

Procedure

Operation	Keyboard Entry	Function Touch	Display	Description
Set decimal to four places				
Clear registers and display		C	0.0000	
Enter 12.7 percent as a decimal	.127	x	0.1270	
Enter 5280	5280	=	670.5600	Answer

Thus 12.7 percent of 5280 is found to be 670.56.

In this problem, we first convert percentage to a decimal, and then multiply that decimal times the base (5280). Since the calculator can handle multiplications so efficiently and rapidly, it is the ideal instrument for figuring percentages.

Percentage Problem

Our next exercise has a little different twist:
What is $24\frac{1}{7}$ percent of 26?

You must first convert $\frac{1}{7}$ to decimal form, combine that decimal with 0.24, and then multiply the combined decimal times 26. Round your answer to three decimal places.

Procedure

Operation	Keyboard Entry	Function Touch	Display	Description
Set decimal to five places				
Clear registers and display		C	0.00000	
Enter numerator of $\frac{1}{7}$	1	÷	1.00000	
Enter denominator of $\frac{1}{7}$ (Remember that we are dealing with $\frac{1}{7}$ of 1 percent.)	700	=	0.00142	
Transfer display to add register	None	+	0.00142	
Enter 24 percent as a decimal	.24	=	0.24142	
Transfer display to multiply register	None	x	0.24142	
Enter 26	26	=	6.27692	Answer

Rounded to three decimal places, 24$\frac{1}{7}$ percent of 26 is 6.277.

DETERMINING PERCENTAGE

Oftentimes we are asked to determine what percentage one number is of another. For example, if we were asked to determine what percentage of 10 is 5, we can tell by looking at the problem that the answer is 50 percent. We simply see that 5 is half of 10—that is, 5/10 (0.5) of 10—or 50 percent of 10. We have made a fraction of the two numbers given, converted that fraction to a decimal equivalent, and then moved the decimal point two places to the right.

Finding Percentage of Two Numbers

How would you solve this problem?
What percentage of 16$\frac{2}{3}$ is 22$\frac{7}{8}$?

$$\text{Percentage} = \frac{22\frac{7}{8}}{16\frac{2}{3}} \times 100$$

Procedure

Operation	Keyboard Entry	Function Touch	Display	Description
Set decimal to five places				
Clear registers and display		C	0.00000	
Enter numerator of $\frac{7}{8}$	7	÷	7.00000	
Enter denominator of $\frac{7}{8}$	8	=	0.87500	
Clear registers and display		C	0.00000	
Enter numberator of 2/3	2	÷	2.00000	
Enter denominator of 2/3	3	=	0.66666	
Clear registers and display		C	0.00000	
Enter numerator of original problem in decimal form	22.875	÷	22.87500	
Enter denominator of original problem in decimal form	16.66666	=	1.37250	
Transfer display to multiply register	None	x	1.37250	
Enter 100	100	=	137.25000	Answer

Rounded off to two places, the answer is 137.25 percent.

PROFIT CALCULATIONS

Industry could not operate in our society without profit, so calculations involving percentage of profit become very important to all business transactions in our lives. Profit can be figured on the selling price, or it may be figured on the purchase price.

If a dealer buys an automobile for $1100, and sells it for $1895, what is the percentage of gross profit on the **selling** price?

Procedure

Operation	Keyboard Entry	Function Touch	Display	Description
Set decimal to four places				
Clear registers and display		C	0.0000	
Enter sales price	1895	+	1895.0000	
Enter purchase price	1100	—	795.0000	Gross profit
Transfer display to divide register	None	=	795.0000	
Enter sales price	1895	÷	0.4195	
Transfer display to multiply register	None	x	0.4195	
Enter percentage conversion factor	100	=	41.9500	Answer

The dealer makes a profit of about 42 percent of the selling price of the automobile.

Percent Profit

A dealer buys an automobile for $1,100, and sells it for $1,895. What is the percentage of gross profit on the **purchase** price?

Procedure

Operation	Keyboard Entry	Function Touch	Display	Description
Set decimal to four places				
Clear registers and display		C	0.0000	
Enter sales price	1895	+	1895.0000	
Enter purchase price	1100	—	795.0000	

Operation	Keyboard Entry	Function Touch	Display	Description
Transfer display to divide register	None	÷	795.0000	
Enter purchase price	1100	=	0.7227	
Transfer display to multiply register	None	÷	0.7227	
Enter percentage conversion factor	100	=	72.2700	

The dealer makes a profit of about 72 percent of the purchase price of the automobile.

Distributing Profit

When partners own a business, the profit is divided in proportion to some prearranged agreement, usually by the percentage of ownership each partner has in the business enterprise. If a company were owned equally by six partners, each partner would be entitled to $16\frac{2}{3}$ percent (one-sixth) of the profit that the company earned. Consider this problem:

The profit on a $985 sale is $22\frac{7}{8}$ percent. Calude's share of the profit is $16\frac{2}{3}$ percent. How much does Claude receive from the sale?

Procedure

Operation	Keyboard Entry	Function Touch	Display	Description
Set decimal to five places				
Clear registers and display		C	0.00000	
Enter numerator of $\frac{2}{3}$	2	÷	2.00000	
Enter denominator of $\frac{2}{3}$ of 1 percent	300	=	0.00666	Decimal form of $\frac{2}{3}$ of 1 percent
Transfer display to add register	None	+	0.00666	
Enter 16 percent as a decimal	.16	=	0.16666	Decimal form of $16\frac{2}{3}$ percent (record)
Clear registers and display		C	0.00000	
Enter numerator of $\frac{7}{8}$	7	÷	7.00000	
Enter denominator of $\frac{7}{8}$ of 1 percent	800	=	0.00875	Decimal form of $\frac{7}{8}$ of 1 percent
Transfer display to add register	None	+	0.00875	
Enter 22 percent as a decimal	.22	=	0.22875	Decimal form of $22\frac{7}{8}$ percent

Operation	Keyboard Entry	Function Touch	Display	Description
Transfer display to multiply register	None	x	0.22875	
Enter amount of sale	985	=	225.31875	Total profit
Transfer display to multiply register	None	x	225.31875	
Enter Claude's share of the profit (expressed as a decimal)	.16666	=	37.55162	Claude's share of the total profit

Rounded off, Claude's share of the profit is $37.55.

LIST PRICE CALCULATIONS

Manufacturers go to great lengths to determine every expense that goes into the manufacture of their products. In addition, profits must be calculated, overhead determined, and list prices suggested. In the following problem, the manufacturer has determined his costs and has set his overhead and profit percentage. He must now consider all other factors that comprise the selling, or list price before he can launch an advertising campaign.

List Price

Wrought Cloth Furniture Factories, Inc., manufactures living room furniture. A certain group costs the factory $670 to manufacture, to which the company must add 85 percent to cover overhead and profit. The distributor adds 15 percent to his cost, and the dealer buys from the distributor at a 40-percent discount from the list price. What will be the list price of the group?

The items included in the list price are (1) manufacturing cost, $670; (2) overhead and profit, 85 percent of $670; (3) distributor's profit, 15 percent of $670 plus 85 percent of $670; and (4) dealer's profit, 40 percent of list price.

The manufacturing cost, the manufacturer's overhead and profit, and the distributor's profit represent 60 percent of the list price.

Procedure

Operation	Keyboard Entry	Function Touch	Display	Description
Set decimal to three places				
Clear registers and display		C	0.000	
Enter manufacturing cost	670	x	670.000	Cost to manufacture

Operation	Keyboard Entry	Function Touch	Display	Description
Enter 85 percent (as decimal)	.85	=	569.500	Overhead and profit (record)
Transfer display to add register	None	+	569.600	
Add cost to manufacture	670	=	1239.500	Cost to manufacture plus overhead and profit (record)
Transfer display to multiply registers	None	x	1239.500	
Enter distributor's percentage (as decimal)	.15	=	185.925	Distributor's profit (record)
Transfer display to add registers	None	+	185.925	
Add cost to manufacture plus overhead and profit (from above)	1239.500	=	1425.425	60 percent of list price
Transfer display to divide register	None	±	1425.425	
Divide display by 60	60	=	23.757	Equals 1 percent of list price
Transfer display to multiply register	None	x	23.757	
Enter 100 (for 100 percent of list price)	100	=	2375.700	List price

The list price of the group is $2,375.70.

MANUFACTURING CONSIDERATIONS

Manufacturers use percentages daily in calculating production costs and design considerations. The problem we will discuss now involves percentages and ratios, and is typical of the many problems facing manufacturing employees.

Word Problem on Percentages

At Shipshape Boat Works, a welder ordered a certain size welding rod from the stockroom. Due to the limited quarters where the task was to be performed, the length of the welding rod had to be limited also. When the welder received the rod from the stockroom, he found it was 20 percent longer than he ordered. He measured it, and found it to be 18 in. long. What length did he order?

In solving this problem, we **cannot** take 20 percent of 18 in., and then subtract the amount from 18 in. to arrive at the answer. The problem states that the rod the welder received was 20 percent longer than the rod he **ordered**, not 20 percent longer than the rod he **received**. If we let the rod ordered

ELDORADO MATHMAGIC—To achieve operational simplicity, the Mathmagic operates algebraically; i.e., its operation is identical to conventional arithmetic. Calculations are entered as they would normally be spoken or written. Although calculations are made to a full 8-digit accuracy, it stores exponents, thus extending its operating range well beyond that of many larger machines. And since there is little likelihood of errors due to underflow or overflow, the need for error or overflow indicators is eliminated.

The Mathmagic is available in two models: Mathmagic A (ac only), and Mathmagic B (ac or dc with internal rechargeable batteries). Either unit features a four-function constant. The answer from any operation or accumulation of operations may be entered as a constant by pressing a single key. The answer from any constant calculation can be used for further calculations without reentry. This is particularly useful for raising to a power, compound interest calculations, nth roots, depreciation calculations, etc.

The Mathmagic has an input of 8 digits, and not only calculates to 8-digit-accuracy, but it stores exponents. With the floating input and output decimal point system, numbers within the range of 1×10^{-20} to 9.9999999×10^{79} can be handled. When negative numbers are displayed, a minus indicator appears to inform the operator. The components of the instrument are MOS / LSI. The unit measures 3½ x 6½ x 1¼ inches, and weighs 16 ounces. **Eldorado Electrodata Corporation, 935 Detroit Avenue, Concord, California 94518.**

represent 100 percent, then the rod received was 120 percent. The problem tells us that 120 percent equals 18 in. We therefore have a ratio:

$$120 \text{ is to } 18 \text{ as } 100 \text{ is to } a$$

or

$$120:18 = 100:a$$

or

$$\frac{120}{18} = \frac{100}{a}$$

In problems involving ratios, we are comparing quantities. If we say one item is half as big as another, we are comparing by the **ratio method**, and we have used a fraction to do so. Here, in this ratio problem, we have said that the fraction 120/18 is equivalent (equal) to the fraction 100/a. The ratio 120/18 is equal to the ratio 100/a.

To solve for **a**, we must isolate **a** to one side of the equation, and we do this by multiplying both sides by the denominators, 18 and **a**.

$$\frac{18(a)120}{18} = \frac{18(a)100}{a}$$

Canceling, we have

$$120\,a = 1800$$

Dividing both sides by 120, we have

$$\frac{120(a)}{120} = \frac{1800}{120}$$

Canceling again, we have

$$a = \frac{1800}{120}$$

It is now a simple matter to solve for **a** on the electronic calculator.

Procedure

Operation	Keyboard Entry	Function Touch	Display	Description
Set decimal to two places				
Clear registers and display		C	0.00	
Enter numerator	1800	+	1800.00	
Enter denominator	120	=	15.00	Answer

The welder ordered a welding rod 15 in. long.

WAGE INCREASES

Wages are important to both the employer and the employee. If the wages are too high, the employer cannot compete in the sale of his products to the consumers. If the wages are too low, the employee cannot maintain an adequate standard of living. The next problem deals with a situation where an employee is receiving a certain wage after he received a percentage increase on his former salary.

Percent and Wages

Jimmy receives a wage of $585.75 a month, after receiving a raise of 6½ percent. What was his wage before his raise?

The 6½ percent raise is 6½ percent of his **old** wage, not his new wage. To solve this problem, we will assign 100 percent as the old wage, and add to that 6½ percent to represent his new wage. Therefore, his new wage equals 106.5 percent of his old wage. Dividing by 100, we eliminate the percentage factor, and find that the new wage equals 1.065 times the old wage.

$$\text{New wage} = 1.065 \times \text{old wage}$$

or

$$\$585.75 = 1.065 \times \text{old wage}$$

Dividing both sides of the equation by 1.065, and canceling, we have

$$\frac{585.75}{1.065} = \text{Old wage}$$

The problem is now easily solved on the calculator.

Procedure

Operation	Keyboard Entry	Function Touch	Display	Description
Set decimal to three places				
Clear registers and display		C	0.00000	
Enter numerator	585.75	±	585.75000	
Enter denominator	1.065	=	550.00000	Answer

Jimmy earned $550.00 a month before his raise.

TIME COMPARISONS

Industries compete with each other in many different ways. The following problem deals only with time comparisons in the completion of a contract, but many other factors are considered in the awarding of contracts. One company may take a much longer time to perform on a contract, but it may be that their price is far more reasonable.

Labor Percentage Calculations

Eager Aerospace Corp. has proposed to build a certain missile system in $11\frac{5}{8}$ mo. A competitor, Bush Airplane Factory, which is a much smaller company, has proposed to build the same system in $36\frac{1}{3}$ mo. Expressed in percentage, how much more time would it take Bush than Eager to fabricate the system?

$$\text{Percent excess} = \frac{\text{Bush's estimate} - \text{Eager's estimate x 100}}{\text{Eager's estimate}}$$

Procedure

Operation	Keyboard Entry	Function Touch	Display	Description
Set decimal to five places				
Clear registers and display		C	0.00000	
Enter Bush's time estimate in decimal form	36.33333	+	36.33333	
Enter Eager's time estimate in decimal form	11.625	−	24.70833	
Transfer display to divide register	None	±	24.70833	
Enter denominator (Eager's estimate in decimal form)	11.625	=	2.12544	
Transfer display to mulitply register	None	x	2.12544	
Enter 100 (to convert to percentage)	100	=	212.54400	Answer

It would take Bush approximately 213 percent more time to build the system than it would take Eager.

PRICE MARKUPS AND MARKDOWNS

On the retail level, merchants must mark up the cost of each item they sell if they are to remain in business. The

VICTOR MODEL MEC 225—The Victor MEC (Miniature Electronic Calculator) Model 225 is a compact unit that is attractively color coordinated, housed in a durable, high-impact Noryl case with a nonglare stipple finish. It measures 8 x 3⅞ inches, and weighs only 20 ounces. The **uni-plane display** features larger, easier-to-read characters in perfect alignment in a single plane; and since the 225 has a 12-digit display capacity, a wider range of calculations can be performed with accuracy and convenience than with the usual 8-digit-capacity unit.

One of the best features of the 225 is its accumulating memory register, which stores any calculated result at the touch of a key. You can add or subtract directly to or from the register. Amounts can be brought out of accumulating register to the main calculating register to be used as desired at the touch of another key. The 225 can be used for automatic constant multiplication and division, as well as automatic repeat addition and subtraction. The grand total is the accumulation of individual results in addition, multiplication, and division in the accumulating memory register.

The unit has recall flexibility to permit recalling of the last displayed amount for use in subsequent computations wihhout reindexing. The underflow system assures accuracy in large addition and multiplication problems by retaining the 12 most significant digits. Rounded answer can be obtained at any one of 10 decimal settings, 0 through 9. **Victor Comptometer Corporation, 3900 N. Rockwell Street, Chicago, Illinois 60618.**

difference between the cost price and the selling price (the markup) pays for the cost of operating the retail establishment, and provides a profit for the owners. During a sale period, merchants commonly mark down their prices from the regular selling price. An item that regularly sells for $100 might be marked down to $80, a savings of $20 to the purchaser. The sale price is 20 percent off the regular price, in this case.

Markup and Markdown

Before Christmas, Bob's Bike Shop marked up its Teamsong Ten-Speed Tandems, which had a wholesale cost of $348, by 40 percent. After Christmas, they marked these bicycles down by 11 percent from the regular selling price, for a special sale. What was the sale price of these bicycles?

Procedure

Operation	Keyboard Entry	Function Touch	Display	Description
Set decimal to three places				
Clear registers and display		C	0.000	
Enter wholesale cost	348	x	348.000	
Enter regular markup rate (40 percent expressed as a decimal	.4	=	139.200	Amount of markup
Transfer display to add register	None	+	139.200	
Enter wholesale cost	348	=	487.200	Regular selling price
Transfer display to multiply register	None	x	487.200	
Enter markdown (11 percent expressed as a decimal)	.11	=	53.592	Amount of markdown (record)
Clear registers and display		C	0.000	
Enter regular selling price	487.20	+	487.200	
Enter amount of markdown (rounded to nearest cent)	53.59	—	433.61	Sale price

The sale price of the bicycle is $433.61. Note that if the amount of the markup is not being calculated, steps can be saved by simply multiplying the cost by 140 percent, which will immediately give the selling price (100 percent of cost price plus 40 percent markup price equals 140 percent, which is 1.4). Multiplying $348 by 1.4 will yield an answer of $487.20. Similarly, the discounted sale price is 100 percent of the regular price less 11 percent markdown, or 89 percent. This percentage, expressed as a decimal, is 0.89. The sale price can be calculated by multiplying the regular price by 0.89, which will give the sale price in one step. Using this procedure, the amount of the markdown will not be calculated.

In order to determine the selling price if the former price of a product is known and the percentage increase is known, we simply multiply the percent increase, expressed as a decimal, times the former price, and then take that product and add it to the former price. If an item that is selling for $100 is to be marked up 20 percent, we determine how much 20 percent of the current selling price is ($20), and add this to the current selling price to arrive at the marked up price ($120).

Price Markup Percentage

A steak that cost $1.25 a pound last month has been marked up 160 percent this month. What is the price of the steak now?

New price = old price plus markup

Procedure

Operation	Keyboard Entry	Function Touch	Display.	Description
Set decimal to three places				
Clear registers and display		C	0.000	
Enter markup percentage expressed as a decimal	1.6	x	1.600	
Enter old price	1.25	=	2.000	Amount of markup
Transfer display to add register	None	+	2.000	
Enter old price	1.25	=	3.250	Answer

The price of the steak this month is $3.25 per pound.

Almost any big-city newspaper on any given day will carry an advertisement something like: "All prices slashed 30 percent." If a customer knows the former price of a particular item in the store that is advertising, he can calculate the new price.

Sale Price Calculation

Cynthia finds that the price of a dress has been marked down 18 percent from the regular price of $19.99. What is the reduced price of the dress?

Procedure

Operation	Keyboard Entry	Function Touch	Display	Description
Set decimal to four places				
Clear registers and display		C	0.0000	
Enter 18 percent as a decimal	.18	x	0.1800	
Enter regular price of dress	19.99	=	3.5982	Price reduction (record)
Clear registers and display		C	0.0000	
Enter regular price of dress	19.99	+	19.9900	
Enter price reduction	3.5982	−	16.3918	Reduced price of dress

The sale price of the dress is $16.39.

A second, and perhaps shorter method of solving this problem follows. If the price of the dress has been reduced 18 percent, then it must sell for 100 percent minus 18 percent, or 82 percent of its regular price.

Procedure

Operation	Keyboard Entry	Function Touch	Display	Description
Set four decimal places				
Clear registers and display		C	0.0000	
Enter percent that dress is selling for (expressed as a decimal)	.82	x	0.8200	
Enter regular price of dress	19.99	=	16.3918	Reduced price of dress

SALES COMMISSION

Thousands of people work only on a commission basis. This means that the amount of pay they receive is a certain prearranged percentage of their total sales. Others, such as department store clerks, work on a salary plus a commission. Still others, such as cab drivers, work on a commission, but the employer guarantees that the employee will be paid a certain minimum amount for each hour worked.

Maria earns a 24⅓ percent commission on a sale of $12,500 worth of merchandise. What is the amount of her commission?

We must convert the percentage figure to decimal form. Since ⅓ equals 0.3333, then 24⅓ % will equal 0.243333. Rounded to three decimal places, the figure we will use in our calculation is 0.243.

Procedure

Operation	Keyboard Entry	Function Touch	Display	Description
Set decimal to three places				
Clear registers and display		C	0.000	
Enter 24-1 / 3 percent in decimal form	.243	x	0.243	
Enter amount of sale	12500	=	3037.500	Answer

Maria's commission is $3,037.50.

DIVERSE PERCENTAGE CALCULATIONS

So many types of percentage calculations exist that it would take volumes to cover them all. We have attempted in this section to explain to the user of electronic calculators how percentage calculations in general are handled. Before moving on to another topic, we will look at several other types of problems that involve percentage calculations.

Blending Profit

Gamma Chocolate Mix Co. blends Alpha chocolate, at a cost of $0.11 per pound, with Beta Chocolate, at a cost of $0.23 per pound, in the ratio of 3 to 1. If the blend is sold at $0.22 per pound, what is the profit percentage on the selling price?

For convenience, we will use 4 lb as the weight of a sample blend (3 lb of Alpha chocolate and 1 lb of Beta chocolate) in these calculations.

Procedure

Operation	Keyboard Entry	Function Touch	Display	Description
Set decimal to four places				
Clear registers and display		C	0.0000	
Enter Alpha cost in cents	11	x	11.0000	
Enter Alpha pounds in 4 lb blend	3	=	33.0000	
Transfer display to add register	None	+	33.0000	Alpha cost in 4 lb sample of blend
Enter Beta cost in cents in 4 lb blend	23	=	56.0000	
Transfer display to divide register	None	±	56.0000	Total cost in 4 lb blend (cents)
Enter weight of sample	4	=	14.0000	Cost of 1 lb blend in cents (record)
Clear registers and display		C	0.0000	
Enter selling price (cents)	22	+	22.0000	
Enter cost per pound	14	−	8.0000	Profit per pound
Transfer display to divide register	None	±	8.0000	
Enter selling price (cents)	22	=	0.3636	
Transfer display to multiply register	None	x	0.3636	
Enter percent conversion factor	100	=	36.36	Answer

The company makes 36.36 percent profit on the selling price of this blend.

Total Income From Percent Saved

In the first 6 months of last year Joanne Ozark saved 11 percent of what she earned. In the second 6 months, she saved $418, which was 28 percent of what she earned in that period. If her total savings for the year were $862, how much was her annual income?

The first step in solving this problem is to determine how much Joanne saved in the first 6 months, since the problem tells us only what she saved during the last 6 months, and the total for the year. Then, if we divide the amount saved each period by the rate (11 percent and 28 percent, respectively), expressed in decimal form, we will know how much Joanne earned in each of those periods. We then only need to add the earnings in the two periods to obtain the annual income.

SUMMIT MOFRL K16—This little mini calculator is a shirt pocket portable weighing only 8¼ ounces and measuring only 2¾ x 4 x 1⅛ in. Its small size permits efficient one-hand operation. It is American made and represents the industry's most advanced technology in design and operation. It is backed by a one-year warranty or over-the-counter exchange. Housed in an attractive break-resistant case, the calculator is fully functional on either ac or dc power. Its built-in ni-cad batteries provide 10 hours of continuous service, and it recharges in only 3 hours. An indicator signals when the batteries are too low to operate the unit efficiently.

The unit has 8-digit entry and readout, with 16-digit floating decimal and calculating capacity. Answers are always decimally correct. Unneeded zeros are automatically suppressed, and special signs indicate signal entry errors, negative answers for true credit balance, and overflow. The large keyboard has finger-contoured keys with a locator dot on the "5" key. Automatic entry overflow protection locks the keyboard to prevent wrong answers. A change sign key permits change of a plus entry to a minus entry and vice versa. Algebraic logic permits multiplying a negative number by a positive number with the correct sign in the answer. In addition to the four basic functions, the unit can be used for mixed and chain calculation.

Each calculator comes with charger and a deluxe padded pouch. **Summit International Corporation, 180 West 2950 South, Salt Lake city, Uath 84115.**

Procedure

Operation	Keyboard Entry	Function Touch	Display	Description
Set decimal to four places				
Clear registers and display		C	0.0000	
Enter annual savings	862	+	862.0000	
Enter last 6 mo savings	418	−	444.0000	First 6 mo savings
Transfer display to dividend register	None	÷	444.0000	
Enter first 6 mo savings rate (11 percent in decimal form)	.11	=	4036.3636	First 6 mo income (record)
Clear registers and display		C	0.0000	
Enter second 6 mo savings	418	÷	418.0000	
Enter second 6 mo savings rate (28 percent in decimal form)	.28	=	1492.8571	Second 6 mo income
Transfer display to add register	None	+	1492.8571	
Enter first 6 mo income	4036.36	+	5529.2171	Answer

Joanne's income last year was $5529.22.

Boy-Girl Relationship

Cynthia says there are 22 other girls in her class. If there are 40 pupils in the class, what percent are boys?

Procedure

Operation	Keyboard Entry	Function Touch	Display	Description
Set decimal to three places				
Clear registers and display		C	0.000	
Enter Cynthia	1	+	1.000	
Enter other girls	22	+	23.000	Girls in class (record)
Clear registers and display		C	0.000	
Enter pupils in class	40	+	40.000	
Enter girls in class	23	−	17.000	Boys in class
Tranfer display to divide register	None	÷	17.000	
Enter pupils in class	40	=	0.425	Boys-to-pupils ratio

Operation	Keyboard Entry	Function Touch	Display	Description
Transfer display to divide register	None	x	0.425	
Enter conversion factor (percents in an entirety)	100	=	42.500	Percent boys in class

Percentage Calculation

Julius picked 182 good cantaloupes in his field, and 44 that he could not sell because they were overripe. What percentage of his crop was marketable? Carry the answer to one decimal place.

Procedure

Operation	Keyboard Entry	Function Touch	Display	Description
Set decimal to four places				
Clear registers and display		C	0.0000	
Enter number of good cantaloupes	182	+	182.0000	
Enter number of over- ripe cantaloupes	44	=	226.0000	Total crop (record)
Clear registers and display		C	0.0000	
Enter number of good cantaloupes	182	÷	182.0000	
Enter total number of cantaloupes	226	=	0.8053	
Transfer display to multiply register	None	x	0.8053	
Multiply by 100 to convert to percent	100	=	80.5300	Answer

Julius could market 80.5 percent of his crop (rounded to one decimal place).

Division and Percentage Word Problem

A certain county reported 2179 marriages and 715 divorces in a 1-year period. What percentage of divorces to marriages occurred in that county? Carry your answer out to one decimal place.

Procedure

Operation	Keyboard Entry	Function Touch	Display	Description
Set decimal to four places				

Operation	Keyboard Entry	Function Touch	Display	Description
Clear registers and display		C	0.0000	
Enter number of divorces	715	÷	715.0000	
Enter number of marriages	2179	x	0.3281	
Multiply times 100 to obtain percentage	100	=	32.8100	Answer (before rounding)

Rounded to one decimal place, the answer is 32.8 percent.

Bankruptcy Calculations

Gee-Haw Horse Products Co. has gone bankrupt. It was found that the company has $82,419.36 in assets, and when these assets are divided proportionally among the creditors, each will receive $0.14 on the dollar ($0.14 for each dollar owed the creditors). What is the total liability to the creditors of the company?

The assets are 14 percent of the liabilities, and will be divided in proportion to the liabilities. If we divide the assets by the liabilities, we have 0.14.

$$\frac{\text{Assets}}{\text{Liabilities}} = 0.14$$

Substituting the known values and cross multiplying, we have

$$\$82,419.36 = 0.14 \text{ x liabilities}$$

or

$$\text{Liabilities} = \frac{\$82,419.36}{0.14}$$

Procedure

Operation	Keyboard Entry	Function Touch	Display	Description
Set decimal to two places				
Clear registers and display		C	0.00	
Enter numerator	82419.36	÷	82419.36	
Enter denominator	.14	=	588709.71	Answer

The company has liabilities in the amount of $588,709.71.

PIECEWORK CALCULATIONS

While thousands of persons work on a commission basis for what they sell, thousands of other workers work on a similar basis for what they **fabricate**. These latter workers are paid a certain amount for each item they make, and are called pieceworkers. Usually, these workers are guaranteed a certain rate of pay, even if for some reason their production is below standard. Some pieceworkers, if they are exceptionally fast, can earn a very good living.

Pete works in a factory where he is paid $0.173 (17.3 cents) for each piece he fabricates. He can fabricate 40 pieces an hour. How long will he have to work to earn $5000? Express the answer in weeks, (assume he works 40 hours a week).

The first step in solving this problem is to determine how much per hour Pete earns. Multiply this by 40 (hours per week) to determine how much he earns per week. Divide his weekly pay into $5000 to find out how many weeks it will take to earn this amount of money.

Procedure

Operation	Keyboard Entry	Function Touch	Display	Description
Set decimal to four places		C		
Clear registers and display		x	0.0000	
Enter amount paid for each piece ($0.173)	.173		0.1730	
Enter number of pieces fabricated per hour	40	x	6.9200	Earnings per hour
Transfer answer to multiply register	None	C	6.9200	
Enter number of hours per work week	40		276.8000	Earnings per week (record)
Clear registers and display			0.0000	
Enter earnings goal	5000		5000.0000	
Enter earnings per week	276.8		18.0635	Answer before rounding

Pete will have to do piecework for 18.064 weeks to earn $5000.

ELEMENTARY ALGEBRA

Algebra is an entire field by itself. It would be impossible for us to present a complete book on algebra within the con-

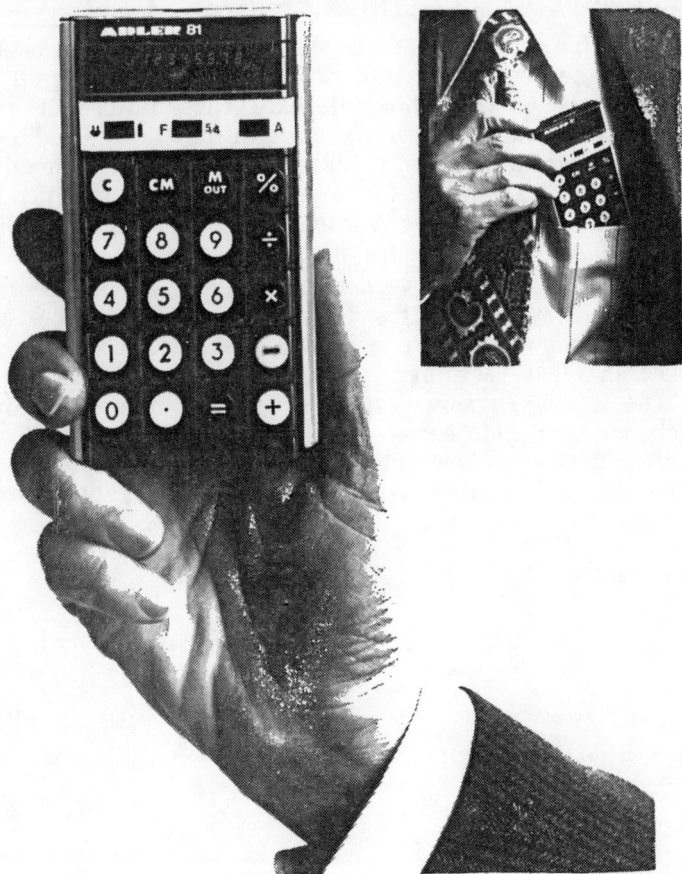

ADLER MODEL 81—A memory is a useful feature in an electronic calculator, and the little Adler Model 81 has one! When grocery shopping, for example, it is possible to put the running total of items purchased into the memory register, and then use the calculator to perform unit pricing. After unit price calculations are complete, simply clear the display, and recall the running total. There are many other times when a memory is helpful.

The 81 is a very versatile, battery operated unit with man-size keys for easy operation, and can be used for computing discounts, sales tax, net amounts, etc. without reentry. There's automatic constant multiplication and division capability built into the instrument. It operates on ac, with a recharger (and ac adpater) included, and is shirt-pocket size.

The unit features an 8-digit light-emitting-diode display, floating-fixed decimal, round-off, percent key, accumulating memory, chain multiplication and division, automatic squaring and raising to a power without reentry, and repeat addition and subtraction. It has a credit balance indicator, an overflow indication, and a zero suppression circuit. **Adler Business Machines, 1600 Route 22, Union, New Jersey 07083.**

fines of this chapter. Instead, we shall merely touch upon a few topics to show how the calculator can be used in solving algebra problems. As you read these elementary problems, you will note that most of the effort in solving each problem seems to be in rearranging the problem for the calculator. By the time we do enter numbers in the keyboard, it seems that 75 percent of the work in solving the problem has been done.

Before algebra problems can be tackled, the student should have a good understanding of basic mathematics, because all four basic mathematical operations (addition, subtraction, multiplication, and division) are employed in algebra problems. Once a student gets used to using letters in place of numbers, and actually solving some of the simple algebra problems, algebra can be fun. In addition to the four basic mathematical operations, algebra employs two other fundamental operations: raising quantities to powers, and extracting roots of quantities. However, we will not get into these two latter areas here.

Combination Word Problem

Together, Lynda and Diane have $18.74. Lynda has $3.70 more than Diane. How much does each of the girls have?

Let us assign the value x to the amount that Lynda has. Therefore, the amount that Diane has is x — $3.70. Then, x (the amount Lynda has) plus x — $3.70 (the amount Diane has) equals $18.74. The problem can be stated as

$$x + x - 3.70 = 18.74$$

or

$$2x - 3.70 = 18.74$$

Transposing, the equation is

$$2x = 18.74 + 3.70$$

or

$$2x = 22.44$$

Dividing each side of the equation by 2, the equation becomes

$$\frac{2x}{2} = \frac{22.44}{2}$$

or

$$x = \frac{22.44}{2}$$

The unknown may be solved by the calculator.

Procedure

Operation	Keyboard Entry	Function Touch	Display	Description
Set decimal to two places				
Clear registers and display		C	0.00	
Enter dividend	22.44	÷	22.44	
Enter divisor	2	=	11.22	Value of x

Lynda has $11.22. Diane has $3.70 less than Lynda, or $11.22 minus $3.70, which is $7.52.

To check the answer, add $11.22 and $7.52. The total is $18.74.

Division Word Problem

At an auction, a salesman bought a lot of goodniks for $1500, and then sold all but 30 of them for $5 each. He obtained $1500 for the goodniks he sold. How many did he buy?

Let x be the number he bought, and x — 30 the number he sold. Multiplying $5 times the number he sold gives us

$$5(x-30)=1500$$

Thus

$$5x-150=1500$$

Transposing

$$5x=1500+150$$

Therefore

$$5x=1650$$

Dividing both sides of the equation by 5 to isolate x

$$x=\frac{1650}{5}$$

Solve for x on the electronic calculator.

Procedure

Operation	Keyboard Entry	Function Touch	Display	Description
Set decimal to 0				
Clear registers and display		C	0	
Enter dividend	1650	÷	1650	
Enter divisor	5	=	330	Answer

To check the answer, multiply $5 times the number sold (330 — 30) to verify that the amount equals $1500.

Division Word Problem

Dan and Marc are 688 miles apart. At exactly 12:00 (noon), each starts driving toward the other. Dan averages 39 mph, and Marc averages 47 mph. At what time will they meet?

The only unknown in this problem is time, which we will assign the letter t. If Marc drives at 47 mph for t hours, then he will drive 688 miles minus the miles that Dan drives.

The problem is stated as

$$47t = 688 - 39t$$

The next step is to move the unknown to one side of the equation, and the known to the other. Transposing, the problem is

$$47t + 39t = 688$$

When we transpose a number from one side of the equation to the other, we must change sign, from plus to minus, or from minus to plus. Therefore, the sign of 39t was changed from a minus to a plus. Combining, we have

$$86t = 688$$

To isolate the unknown, t, to one side, we must divide both sides by 86.

$$\frac{86t}{86} = \frac{688}{86}$$

By canceling, we arrive at

$$t = \frac{688}{86}$$

The unknown, t, is easily found by the calculator.

Procedure

Operation	Keyboard Entry	Function Touch	Display	Description
Set decimal to two places				
Clear registers and display		C	0.00	
Enter dividend	688	÷	688.00	
Enter divisor	86	=	8.00	$t = 8$

Since t equals 8 hours, the boys will meet 8 hours after noon, or at 8:00 p.m.

We can determine the number of miles each drives, by multiplying the average speed times 8. Marc will drive 47 times 8, or 376 mi, and Dan will drive 39 times 8, or 312 mi. To check the answer, we add 376 and 312, which gives us 688 mi, thus proving the answer.

Addition and Multiplication

Wheeler and his partner Dealer went to Hong Kong on a business trip. It took one-third of their money for the airplane fare. They purchased merchandise with half of their money. Other expenses amounted to $1139, and they returned home with $966. How much did they leave with?

We will assign the value x to the amount Wheeler and Dealer left with. The airplane fare is one-third x, the merchandise is one-half x, and the resulting equation is

$$x - \frac{1}{3}x - \frac{1}{2}x - 1139 = 966$$

Transposing, the equation becomes

$$x - \frac{1}{3}x - \frac{1}{2}x = 966 + 1139$$

Next, we find the lowest common denominator for the fractions, and combine

$$\frac{6x}{6} - \frac{2x}{6} - \frac{3x}{6} = 2105$$

and

$$\frac{1x}{6} = 2105$$

To eliminate the fraction, we multiply both sides by 6 using the electronic calculator.

Procedure

Operation	Keyboard Entry	Function Touch	Display	Description
Set decimal to two places				
Clear registers and display		C	0.00	
Enter 6	6	x	6.00	
Enter 2105	2105	=	12630.00	Value of x

Wheeler and Dealer left with $12,630.00.

TEMPERATURE CONVERSIONS

There are four major temperature scales in use throughout the world, Fahrenheit, Celsius, Kelvin, and Rankine.

The Fahrenheit scale was designed by Gabriel Fahrenheit (1686-1736), a German physicist. He mixed equal quantities by weight of common table salt and snow, and assigned zero to the resulting temperature. The freezing point of water is 32, and the boiling point of water is 212 degrees on the Fahrenheit scale.

On the Celsius (formerly **centigrade**) scale, zero represents the freezing point of water, and 100 represents the boiling point.

The Kelvin scale was designed by William Kelvin (1824-1907), a British mathematician and physicist. On this scale, the unit of measure equals the degree on the Celsius scale, but zero on the Kelvin scale is **absolute** zero, or —273.16 degrees Celsius.

The Rankine scale was developed by William Rankine, an engineer and physicist. The unit of measure on this scale is the same as the degree on the Fahrenheit scale, except that the boiling point of water is 671.69, and the freezing point is 491.69. Zero on the Rankine scale also is absolute zero.

Temperature Conversion from Fahrenheit

Convert 115 degrees Fahrenheit to Celsius (C), to Kelvin (K), and to Rankine (R) temperatures.

The temperature conversion formulas needed here are

$$C = (F - 32) / 1.8$$

$$K = C + 273$$
$$R = F + 459.4$$

Procedure

Operation	Keyboard Entry	Function Touch	Display	Description
Set decimal to two places				
Clear registers and display		C	0.00	
Enter temperature in ^{0}F	115	+	115.00	
Enter scale adjustment	32	−	83.00	
Transfer display to divide register	None	÷	83.00	
Enter conversion factor	1.8	=	46.11	Temperature in ^{0}C (record answer)
Transfer display to add register	None	+	46.11	
Enter scale adjustment	273	+	319.11	Temperature in ^{0}K (record answer)
Clear registers and display		C	0.00	
Enter temperature in ^{0}F	115	+	115.00	
Enter scale adjustment	459.4	+	574.40	Temperature in ^{0}R (record answer)

Temperature Conversion from Centigrade

Convert 20 degrees Celsius to Fahrenheit (F), to Kelvin (K), and to Rankine (R) temperature scales.
The necessary equations are

$$F = 1.8C + 32$$
$$K = C + 273$$
$$R = F + 459.4$$

Procedure

Operation	Keyboard Entry	Function Touch	Display	Description
Set decimal to one place				
Clear registers and display		C	0.0	
Enter temperature in oC	20	x	20.0	
Enter conversion factor	1.8	=	36.0	
Transfer display to add register	None	+	36.0	
Enter scale adjustment	32	+	68.0	Temperature in ^{0}F (record answer)

Operation	Keyboard Entry	Function Touch	Display	Description
Enter Rankine scale adjustment	459.4	+	527.4	Temperature in ^{o}R (record answer)
Clear registers and display		C	0.0	
Enter temperature in oC	20	+	20.0	
Enter scale adjustment	273	+	293.0	Temperature in ^{o}K (record answer)

A temperature of 20 degrees Celsius is the same as 68 degrees Fahrenheit, 293 degrees Kelvin, or 527.4 degrees Rankine.

Temperature Conversion from Kelvin

Convert 300 degrees Kelvin to Celsius (C), to Fahrenheit (F), and to Rankine (R) temperature scales.

The formulas necessary for this problem are

$$C = K - 273$$
$$F = 1.8 C + 32$$
$$R = F + 459.4$$

Procedure

Operation	Keyboard Entry	Function Touch	Display	Description
Set decimal to one place				
Clear registers and display		C	0.0	
Enter temperature in oK	300	+	300.0	
Enter scale adjustment	273	−	27.0	Temperature in ^{o}C (record answer)
Transfer display to multiply register	none	x	27.0	
Enter conversion factor	1.8	=	48.6	
Transfer display to add register	None	+	48.6	
Enter Fahrenheit adjustment	32	+	80.6	Temperature in ^{o}F (record answer)
Enter scale adjustment	459.4	+	540.0	Temperature in ^{o}R (record answer)

A temperature of 300 degrees Kelvin is the same as 27 degrees Celsius, 80.6 degrees Fahrenheit, or 540 degrees Rankine.

SUMMIT MODEL SM8—One of the smallest electronic calculators ever made has recently been introduced by Summit International Corporation. It is priced at under $60, and is designed for career men and women, housewives, and students. The SM8 has most of the features found only in larger, more expensive models. It measures just 3⅜ x 2⅛ x ⅞ inches, and offers 8-digit entry and readout, full floating decimal, large keyboard, simple algebraic logic, automatic keyboard constant in all functions, and will add, subtract, multiply, and divide even in chain and mixed calculations. The company considers the SM8 as a significant development in the electronic calculator industry—one that is expected to win the approval of the general user. The unit is sold with a long-lasting disposable battery, stylish carrying pouch, and a one-year factory warranty.

The unit is about the same size as a pack of cigarettes; it is lightweight, and the keyboard is easy to operate despite its small size. **Summit International Corporation, 180 West 2950 South, Salt Lake City, Utah 84115.**

Temperature Conversion from Rankine

Convert 500 degrees Rankine to Celsius (C), to Fahrenheit (F), and to Kelvin (K) temperature scales.
The equations needed in this problem are

$$C = (R - 491.4) / 1.8$$
$$F = R - 459.4$$
$$K = C + 273$$

Procedure

Operation	Keyboard Entry	Function Touch	Display	Description
Set decimal to two places				
Clear registers and display		C	0.00	
Enter temperature in oR	500	+	500.00	
Enter scale adjustment	491.4	−	8.60	
Transfer display to dividend register	None	÷	8.60	
Enter conversion factor	1.8	=	4.78	Temperature in °C (record answer)
Transfer display to add register	None	+	4.78	
Enter scale adjustment	273	+	277.78	Temperature in °K (record answer)
Clear registers and display		C	0.00	
Enter temperature in oR	500	+	500.00	
Enter scale adjustment	459.4	−	40.6	Temperature in °F (record answer)

A temperature of 500 degrees Rankine is the same as 4.8 degrees Celsius, 40.6 degrees Fahrenheit, or 277.8 degrees Kelvin.

4

Fractions

Without a good understanding of fractions, one does not have a good understanding of mathematics itself. We are exposed to fractions in some way almost every day. Mathematics is an exact science, and as such must employ some method to identify parts of wholes—the use of fractions is that method. In our weekly grocery shopping, many items are priced at a whole number of cents and a fraction of a cent, such as 4½ cents per pound. The price is not 5 cents, and it is not 4 cents— it is **exactly** 4½ cents.

It is not particularly difficult to acquire a reasonable skill in the use of fractions. When using an electronic calculator, it is generally wise to convert fractions to **decimal equivalents** (sometimes called **decimal fractions**) before attempting to solve a problem. This chapter contains a number of sample problems and their solutions on the calculator. It begins with a few exercises in converting fractions to decimal numbers, and then continues through addition, subtraction, multiplication, and division fractions. Finally, there are some word problems related to situations that some of us have encountered, or will encounter, during our lives. We have included a problem about an airliner that crashed—we certainly hope that none of you experience an incident such as that!

KINDS OF FRACTIONS

We have stated that a part of a unit is called a fraction, but there are two ways of expressing a fraction. One is as a **common fraction** such as ½, ⅝, $^{77}/_{100}$, etc., and the other is a **decimal fraction** such as 0.5, 0.625, 0.77, etc. By its nature, each expression indicates division.

The fraction itself is made up of two parts, the numerator (the portion of the fraction above the line), and the denominator (the portion below the line). In the decimal fraction, the portion of the fraction below the line is not shown, but is indicated by the location of the decimal point. For example, 0.5 is the same as 5 / 10, 0.625 the same as 625 / 1000, 0.77 the same as 77 / 100, etc. Three other terms associated with fractions are **proper**, **improper**, and **mixed**. A proper fraction means that the number above the line (the numerator) is smaller than the number below the line (the denominator). An improper fraction means that the numerator is larger than the denominator. A mixed number is one in which there is a whole number and a fraction, such as $5\frac{1}{2}$ or $4\,{}^{13}/_{77}$

We have stated that a fraction indicates division. The fraction $\frac{4}{5}$ means $4 \div 5$, and if we carry out the indicated division, we will have as a result a decimal fraction ($4 \div 5 = 0.8$). The decimal fraction itself indicates division, since it is expressed as $8/10$. If division is performed on an improper fraction, we can obtain a mixed number, or if carried a step further, a whole number and a decimal. For example, $3/2$ equals $1\frac{1}{2}$ or 1.5. Conversely, a mixed number can be changed to an improper fraction by multiplying the denominator by the whole number, and adding the numerator to the product to form the numerator in the improper fraction. The denominator is not changed. The mixed number $4\frac{1}{3}$ is changed to an improper fraction by multiplying 3 (the denominator) times 4 (the whole number) and adding 1 (the numerator) to obtain the numerator of the improper fraction (13). Since we do not change the denominator, the improper fraction is $13/3$.

If the numerator and the denominator are both multiplied (or divided) by the same number, the value of the fraction remains unchanged. Thus, the fraction $2/3$ can be changed to an equivalent fraction such as $4/6$ simply by multiplying both parts of the fraction by 2. The fraction $15/25$ can be changed to $3/5$ by dividing the numerator and the denominator by 5. Both fractions ($15/25$ and $3/5$) are equal. When we express a fraction in its lowest terms, we are saying that there is no number that can be further divided into both the numerator and the denominator. The fraction $15/25$ is not expressed in its lowest terms, because we can divide both the numerator and the denominator by another number, 5, to obtain $3/5$. The fraction $3/5$ is expressed in its lowest terms, because there is not any whole number that can be divided into both the numerator and denominator.

LOWEST COMMON DENOMINATOR

There are many times when we do not wish to express a fraction in its lowest terms. If we are adding the fractions $\frac{1}{2}$ and $\frac{1}{4}$, we must first convert to what is called a **common denominator**; that is, the denominator in both fractions must be equal. If we multiply the numerator and the denominator of the fraction $\frac{1}{2}$ by the number 2, we will have the equivalent fraction 2 / 4. It is now possible to add 2 / 4 and 1 / 4 to obtain 3 / 4. In using the electronic calculator, it is convenient to convert common fractions to decimal equivalents before performing the indicated operations.

The **lowest common denominator**, or l.c.d. is a term used with more than one common fraction. If we have two or more fractions, and we wish to convert them to similar fractions— fractions with a common denominator—it is usually desirable to use the lowest number possible as the denominator common to both fractions. In the example previously given, the fractions 1 / 2 and 1 / 4 could have been changed to 4 / 8 and 2 / 8, but 8 would not be the **lowest** common denominator. It is true that 8 is a common denominator, but when we begin to perform mathematical operations with these fractions (4 / 8 and 2 / 8), we find that we are dealing with larger and more cumbersome numbers than is necessary. We are usually much better off using the lowest common denominator. Often, the l.c.d. can be determined by inspection, but it is possible to experiment to arrive at the l.c.d.

CONVERTING FRACTIONS TO DECIMAL EQUIVALENTS

We have previously stated that it is convenient to convert fractions to decimal equivalents when we are using the electronic calculator to perform mathematical operations. To divide 5 / 8 by 3 \ 16 requires several steps using conventional methods, but the operation is relatively simple if we first convert the fractions to decimals, and then carry out the division. If we are required to express the answer in common fraction form instead of decimal fraction form, there is the necessity of converting the decimal answer back into fractions.

Since it is important to understand now to convert common fractions to decimals for use in the electronic calculator, we have included 12 exercises in this operation. The solution to four of these exercises has been given. After you have done the first 4, it would be wise to continue through the rest of the 12 exercises, and then check the answers with the 12 answers given at the conclusion of the problem.

Exercises in Converting Fractions to Decimal Numbers

Convert the following fractions to decimals. Express your answer to each exercise to four decimal places.

1. $\frac{1}{2}$ 3. $\frac{7}{8}$ 5. $\frac{3}{4}$ 7. $\frac{1}{4}$ 9. $\frac{5}{6}$ 11. $\frac{3}{11}$

2. $\frac{1}{3}$ 4. $\frac{1}{8}$ 6. $\frac{2}{7}$ 8. $\frac{2}{5}$ 10. $\frac{4}{9}$ 12. $\frac{23}{64}$

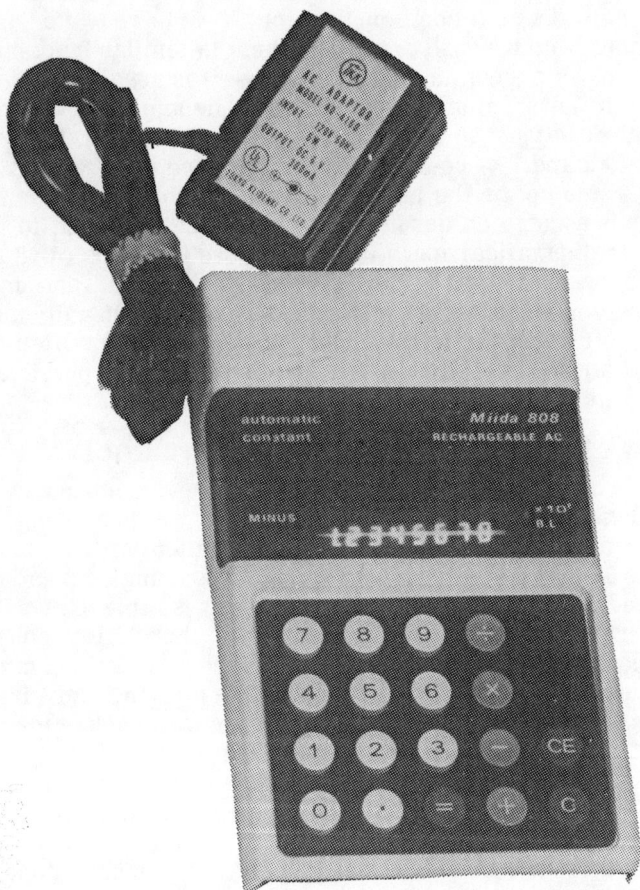

MIIDA MODEL 808—The 808 features an 8-digit oversized display for viewing ease. It will handle addition, subtraction, multiplication, and division, as well as automatic constant calculations. The floating decimal system permits automatic placement of the decimal in the results of the calculations. The unit can be used for figuring percentages and discounts.

Using 4 long-lasting ni-cad batteries, the instrument will provide 4½ hours of continuous operation, at which time the batteries can be recharged. The positive charge (no variable) eliminates malfunctions due to weak or dying batteries. **Miida Electronics, Inc., 2 Hammarskjold Plaza, New York, N.Y. 10017.**

Procedure

Operation	Keyboard Entry	Function Touch	Display	Description
Set decimal to five places				
Clear registers and display		C	0.00000	
Enter numerator of exercise 1	1	÷	1.00000	
Enter denominator of exercise 1	2	=	0.50000	Answer to exercise 1
Clear registers and display		C	0.00000	
Enter numerator of exercise 2	1	÷	1.00000	
Enter denominator of exercise 2	3	=	0.33333	Answer to exercise 2
Clear registers and display		C	0.00000	
Enter numerator of exercise 3	7	÷	7.00000	
Enter denominator of exercise 3	8	=	0.87500	Answer to exercise 3
Clear registers and display		C	0.00000	
Enter numerator of exercise 4	1	÷	1.00000	
Enter denominator of exercise 4	8	=	0.12500	Answer to exercise 4

The remaining exercises are calculated in the same manner. The answers to the exercises are as follows (rounded to four decimal places):

1.	0.5000	5.	0.7500	9.	0.8333
2.	0.3333	6.	0.2857	10.	0.4444
3.	0.8750	7.	0.2500	11.	0.2727
4.	0.1250	8.	0.4000	12.	0.3594

CONVERTING DECIMALS TO COMMON FRACTIONS

We must be as proficient in changing decimal fractions to common fractions as we are in changing common fractions to decimal equivalents. Only one example is given here, but the conversion is the same with any decimal fraction. After you have mastered the procedure, practice with a few other decimal fractions before proceeding with the balance of this chapter.

Decimal to Common Fraction

Express the decimal 0.125 in common fraction form.

From our earlier discussion, we know that 0.125 is the same as $125/1000$, so in order to convert the decimal to a fraction, our first step is to create a common fraction from the decimal fraction given. The next step is to reduce the common fraction just created to its lowest terms. Upon inspection, it is obvious that the number 5 will divide into both 125 and 1000. Further, although not quite so obvious, we can tell that 25 will divide into both the numerator and the denominator. Let us use 25 first and see what we get.

Procedure

Operation	Keyboard Entry	Function Touch	Display	Description
Set decimal to three places				
Clear registers and display		C	0.000	Guard figures
Enter numerator	125	÷	125.000	
Enter 25	25	=	5.000	New numerator
Clear registers and display		C	0.000	
Enter denominator	1000	÷	1000.000	
Enter 25	25	=	40.000	New denominator

We now have a new equivalent fraction, 5/40, which can be further reduced. However, at this point we can perform the calculations mentally by dividing 5 into both the numerator and the denominator, and we will obtain a fraction which **cannot** be further reduced. Thus, the decimal 0.125 is equivalent to the common fraction ⅛.

ADDING FRACTIONS

This section contains several exercises on adding common fractions, and adding mixed numbers, fractions, and decimal fractions. The first problem includes a method of converting decimals back to fractions, which varies somewhat from the previous conversion exercise.

Adding Fractions with the Calculator

Perform the following addition:

$$1/3 + 7/8 + 1/8 + 3/4 + 1/4 + 3/8 + 1/2 + 5/8 = \ ?$$

It is possible to find the l.c.d. and add the numerators on the electronic calculator. Another way, which is illustrated here, is to convert all the fractions to decimal form, and then add the decimal forms on the electronic calculator. The decimal answer may then be converted back to fraction form.

Procedure

Operation	Keyboard Entry	Function Touch	Display	Description
Set decimal to seven places				
Clear registers and display		C	0.0000000	
Enter numerator of 1 / 3	1	÷	1.0000000	
Enter denominator of 1 / 3	3	=	0.3333333	Decimal form of 1/3 (record)
Clear registers and display		C	0.0000000	
Enter numerator of 7 · 8	7	=	7.0000000	
Enter denominator of 7 · 8	8	÷	0.8750000	Decimal form of 7/8 (record)
Clear registers and display		C	0.0000000	
Enter numerator of 1 / 8	1	÷	1.0000000	
Enter denominator of 1 8	8	=	0.1250000	Decimal form of 1/8 (record)

Continue this procedure until the decimal forms of each of the fractions given in the problem have been calculated. These forms are as follows:

$$1/3 = 0.3333333$$

$$7/8 = 0.8750000$$

$$1/8 = 0.1250000$$

$$3/4 = 0.7500000$$

$$1/4 = 0.2500000$$

$$3/8 = 0.3750000$$

$$1/2 = 0.5000000$$

$$5/8 = 0.6250000$$

After the decimal forms have been calculated, the decimals are added as follows:

Procedure

Operation	Keyboard Entry	Function Touch	Display	Description
Clear registers and display		C	0.0000000	

Operation	Keyboard Entry	Function Touch	Display	Description
Enter decimal form of 1 / 3	0.3333333	+	0.3333333	
Enter decimal form of 7 / 8	.875	+	1.2083333	Running total
Enter decimal form of 1 / 8	.125	+	1.3333333	Running total
Enter decimal form of 3 / 4	.75	+	2.0833333	Running total
Enter decimal form of 1 / 4	.25	+	2.3333333	Running total
Enter decimal form of 3 / 8	.375	+	2.7083333	Running total
Enter decimal form of 1 / 2	.5	+	3.2083333	Running total
Enter decimal form of 5 / 8	.625	=	3.8333333	Sum total (record)

The display is the answer in decimal form, but this must be converted to fractional form to correctly answer the problem. We must find the l.c.d. of the fractions, which is usually accomplished by inspection. In this case, the l.c.d. is not easily determined by inspection, so we must experiment. The denominators are the numbers 2, 3, 4, and 8. By experimentation, we find that the lowest number into which each of the denominators can be divided into is 24. Therefore, 24 will be chosen as the l.c.d., even though we may be able to reduce the resulting fraction (as determined by further calculation below) to an even smaller denominator. In this example, the procedure for converting the decimal to a fraction is as follows:

Procedure

Operation	Keyboard Entry	Function Touch	Display	Description
Set decimal to six places				
Clear registers and display		C	0.000000	
Enter l.c.d. as determined by experimentation	24	x	24.000000	Number of 24ths in whole
Enter fractional part of answer, rounded to six places	.833333	=	19.999992	Number of 24ths in fractional part of answer

Rounding off the last display, we find that there are twenty 24ths in the fractional part of our answer. This reduces to $5/6$, making our answer $3 \, 5/6$.

Adding Mixed Fractions and Decimals

Find the sum of the following numbers rounded to 3 decimal places:

$$1\,\tfrac{1}{3} + 2\tfrac{7}{8} + 3.45 + 6\,\tfrac{9}{10} + 11\tfrac{12}{13} + \tfrac{1415}{161}\,?$$

To solve this problem, we must first convert all fractions to decimal equivalents, and then add the decimals on the calculator.

Procedure

Operation	Keyboard Entry	Function Touch	Display	Description
Set decimal to four places				
Clear registers and display		C	0.0000	
Enter numerator of 1/3 (the whole number will be added later)	1	÷	1.0000	
Enter denominator of 1/3	3	=	0.3333	Decimal equivalent of 1/3 (record)
Clear registers and display		C	0.0000	
Enter numerator of 7/8	7	÷	7.0000	
Enter denominator of 7/8	8	=	0.8750	Decimal equivalent of 7/8 (record)
Clear registers and display		C	0.0000	
Enter numerator of 9/10	9	÷	9.0000	Decimal equivalent of 9/10 (record)
Enter denominator of 9/10	10	=	0.9000	
Clear registers and display		C	0.0000	
Enter numerator of 12/13	13	÷	12.0000	
Enter denominator of 12/13	13	=	0.9230	Decimal equivalent of 12/13 (record)
Clear registers and display		C	0.0000	
Enter numerator of 1415/161	1415	÷	1415.0000	
Enter denominator of 1415/161	161	=	8.7888	Decimal equivalent of 1415/161 (record)
Clear registers and display		C	0.0000	
Enter whole numbers of problem	1	+	1.0000	
	2	+	3.0000	Running total
	3	+	6.0000	Running total
	6	+	12.0000	Running total
	11	+	23.0000	Running total
Enter decimal equivalent of 1/3	.3333	+	23.3333	Running total
Enter decimal equivalent of 7/8	.875	+	24.2083	Running total

Operation	Keyboard Entry	Function Touch	Display	Description
Enter decimal from third number in problem set	.45	+	24.6583	Running total
Enter decimal equivalent of 9/10	.9	+	25.5583	Running total
Enter decimal equivalent of 12/13	.923	+	26.4813	Running total
Enter decimal equivalent of 1415/161	8.7888	=	35.2701	Total

Rounded off as required, the answer is 35.270.

SUBTRACTION FRACTIONS

Without an electronic calculator, the usual method of finding the difference betwwen two proper fractions is to change to fractions with an l.c.d., and then subtract the resulting numerators, placing the difference over the l.c.d. With fractions such as those in this problem, it may be much easier to solve the problem in that manner, but as equations become more complex, we find that by using the electronic calculator these complex problems become simple. By changing the fractions to decimal equivalents and subtracting one decimal equivalent from the other, we are able to arrive at the solution. However, the answer must be expressed in fractional form, if it is obvious the problem calls for such an answer.

Solve the following problem:

$$1/3 - 1/8 = ?$$

Procedure

Operation	Keyboard Entry	Function Touch	Display	Description
Set decimal to six places				
Clear registers and display		C	0.000000	
Enter numerator of 1/3	1	÷	1.000000	
Enter denominator of 1/3	3	=	0.333333	Decimal equivalent of 1/3 (record)
Clear registers and display		C	0.000000	
Enter numerator of 1/8	1	÷	1.000000	
Enter denominator of 1/8	8	=	0.125000	Decimal equivalent of 1/8 (record)

Operation	Keyboard Entry	Function Touch	Display	Description
Clear registers and display		C	0.000000	
Enter decimal equivalent of 1/3	.333333	—	0.333333	
Enter decimal equivalent of 1/8	.125	=	0.208333	Answer in decimal form

The answer in decimal form, 0.208333, must be expressed in fractional form, and the fractional form expressed in the lowest common denominator. In most problems, it is possible to find a common denominator, although not necessarily the lowest common denominator, by multiplying the denominators in the problem together. It is sometimes easier to obtain an answer in this manner, and then reduce the fraction thus obtained to the l.c.d. In this problem, multiplying the denominators $(8 \times 3 = 24)$ does produce the l.c.d.

The procedure for converting the decimal answer to a fraction is as follows:

Operation	Keyboard Entry	Function Touch	Display	Description
Clear registers and display		C	0.000000	
Enter l.c.d. as determined above	24	x	24.000000	Number of 24ths in whole
Enter decimal answer	.208333	=	4.999992	Numer of 24ths in decimal answer

Rounding off, we find that we have five 24ths in the decimal answer. The answer, expressed in fractional form, is therefore 5/24.

Subtracting Mixed Numbers

Solve the following problem:

$$6\text{-}^4/_{11} - 4\ ^9/_{17} = ?$$

This problem is similar to the preceding problem, except that the parts of the problem contain a fraction and a whole number. The difference between mixed numbers can be obtained in three different manners. In the problem, $4\frac{1}{3} - 2\frac{1}{2} = ?$, for example, the first method (and the most commonly used) would be to determine the lowest common denominator, which is 6, and state the problem as mixed numbers

$$4\frac{1}{3} = \ 4\frac{2}{6} = 3\frac{8}{6}$$
$$-2\ \frac{1}{5} = -2\frac{3}{6} = -2\frac{3}{6}$$
$$\overline{\hphantom{-2\ \frac{1}{5} = -2\frac{3}{6} =}\ 1\frac{5}{6}}$$

The second method is to convert both parts of the problem to improper fractions

$$4\,^1/_3 \;=\; 4\,^2/_6 \;=\; {}^{26}/_6$$
$$-2\,^1/_2 \;=\; -2\,^3/_6 \;=\; -\,{}^{15}/_6$$
$$\rule{2cm}{0.4pt}$$
$$^{11}/_6 \;=\; 1\,^5/_6$$

The third method, which we will use with the electronic calculator, is to convert the fractions to decimal form, perform the subtract operation, and then convert the decimal back to fractional form

$$4\,^1/_3 \;=\; 4.333333$$
$$-2\,^1/_2 \;=\; -2.500000$$
$$\rule{2cm}{0.4pt}$$
$$1.833333 = 1\,^5/_6$$

Procedure

Operation	Keyboard Entry	Function Touch	Display	Description
Set decimal to six places				
Clear registers and display		C	0.000000	
Enter numerator of 4 / 11	4	÷	4.000000	
Enter denominator of 4 / 11	11	=	0.363636	Decimal form of 4 / 11
Clear registers and display		C	0.000000	
Enter numerator of 9 / 17	9	÷	9.000000	
Enter denominator of 9 / 17	17	=	0.529411	Decimal form of 9 / 17
Clear registers and display		C	0.000000	
Enter 6-4 / 11 in decimal form	6.363636	+	6.363636	
Enter 4-9 / 17 in decimal form	4.529411	–	1.834225	Answer in decimal form
Clear registers and display		C	0.000000	
Set decimal to five places				
Enter denominator of 4 / 11	11	x	11.000000	
Enter denominator of 9 / 17	17	=	187.000000	Common denominator
Transfer display to multiply register		x	187.000000	Number of 187ths in a whole
Enter decimal answer from above, rounded to five places; omitting whole number	.83423	=	156.00101	Number of 187ths in decimal portion of answer

Rounding off, and adding the whole number omitted in the last step, our answer becomes $1\,^{156}/_{187}$. This fraction cannot be reduced, so 187 is the l.c.d.

MULTIPLYING FRACTIONS

The following exercises demonstrate how easy it is to multiply fractions on the electronic calculator.

To multiply a fraction by a fraction, simply multiply the numerators together to form the numerator of the answer, and multiply the denominators together to form the denominator of the answer. Then reduce the answer to its lowest terms. When more than two fractions are involved, as in the next problem, multiply the product of the first two numerators by the third numerator, and that product by the fourth, etc., until all numerators have been multiplied together. The final product is the numerator of the answer. The same procedure holds true for the denominators.

Perform the following multiplication:

$$17/38 \ \text{x} \ 13/84 \ \text{x} \ 1/2 \ =?$$

Procedure

Operation	Keyboard Entry	Function Touch	Display	Description
Set decimal to zero places				
Clear registers and display		C	0	
Enter first numerator	17	x	17	
Enter second numerator	13	x	221	
Enter third numerator	1	=	221	Numerator of answer (record)
Clear registers and display		C	0	
Enter first denominator	38	x	38	
Enter second denominator	84	x	3192	
Enter third denominator	2	=	6384	Denominator of answer

The answer is 221/6384, which cannot be reduced to lower terms.

Multiplying Mixed Fractions

Solve the following problem:

$$6\tfrac{7}{8} \ \text{x} \ 18\tfrac{5}{8} \ = \ ?$$

This problem is similar to the preceding problem, and is solved in the same manner, except that we must first convert the mixed fractions to improper fractions. To obtain the numerator in a mixed fraction, we multiply the denominator times the whole number and add to that product the numerator of the fraction. After converting the mixed frac-

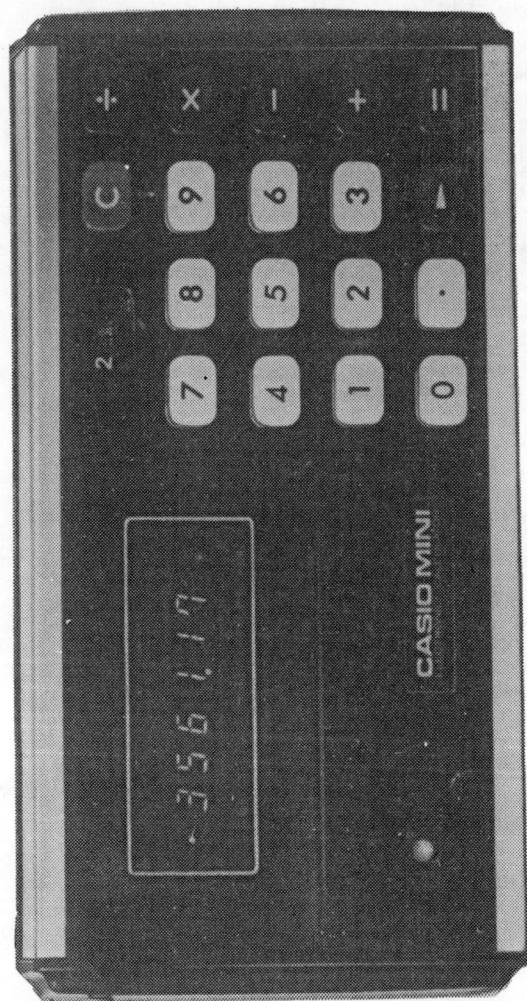

CASIO-MINI MODEL—The manufacturer claims this unit to be the world's best selling electronic calculator. It is low in price, and operates approximately 12 hours continuously with alkaline batteries, or on house current with an optional ac adapter. It will perform addition, subtraction, multiplication, division, chain multiplication and division, square, mixed calculations, and calculations involving decimal places. It's capacity is limited to 6 digits for all inputs, but the product and the quotient can be as large as 12 digits using the unit's double-length display system. The fixed decimal point can be set at either 0 or 2 places.

The unit features credit balance operation, indicated by a minus sign in addition and subtraction problems, and an overflow check, indicated by 0 or 0.00 on the display, locking the calculator.

The instrument measures 1½ x 6 x 3¼ inches, and weighs 12 ounces (including batteries). **Casio, Inc., Suite 4011, One World Trade Center, New York, N.Y. 10048.**

tions to improper fractions, we multiply the numerators together to find the numerator of the answer, and the denominators together to find the denominator of the answer. The answer thus obtained will generally be an improper fraction, and must be converted to a mixed fraction and reduced to its lowest terms.

Procedure

Operation	Keyboard Entry	Function Touch	Display	Description
Set decimal to zero places				
Clear registers and display		C	0	
Enter denominator of first mixed fraction	8	x	8	
Enter whole number of first mixed fraction	6	=	48	
Transfer display to add register	None	+	48	
Add numerator of first mixed fraction	7	=	55	Numerator of first improper fraction (record)
Clear registers and display		C	0	
Enter denominator of second mixed fraction	8	x	8	
Enter whole number of second mixed fraction	18	=	144	
Transfer display to add register	None	+	144	
Enter numerator of second mixed fraction	5	=	149	Numerator of second improper fraction (record)

We now have determined the numerators of the two improper fractions. Since the denominators have not changed, we can now restate the problem as

$$55/8 \times 149/8 = ?$$

We now multiply the numerator together to find the numerator of the answer, and the denominators together to find the denominator of the answer.

Operation	Keyboard Entry	Function Touch	Display	Description
Clear registers and display		C	0	
Enter numerator of first improper fraction	55	x	55	

Operation	Keyboard Entry	Function Touch	Display	Description
Enter numerator of second improper fraction	149	=	8195	Numerator of answer, as improper fraction (record)
Clear registers and display		C	0	
Enter denominator of first improper fraction	8	x	8	
Enter denominator of second improper fraction	8	=	64	Denominator of answer (record)

We have now determined the numerator and the denominator of the answer. However, the result of multiplying two improper fractions is another improper fraction. We must now convert this improper fraction to a mixed fraction. This is accomplished by dividing the denominator into the numerator to produce an answer in decimal form. The decimal form is then converted to a mixed fraction.

Procedure

Operation	Keyboard Entry	Function Touch	Display	Description
Set decimal to four places				
Clear registers and display		C	0.0000	
Enter numerator of answer (improper fraction above)	8195	÷	8195.0000	
Enter denominator of answer (improper fraction above)	64	=	128.0468	Answer in decimal form (record)
Clear registers and display		C	0.0000	
Enter decimal part of answer just obtained	.0468	x	0.0468	Decimal of fraction only
Enter denominator	64	=	2.9952	Numerator of fraction only

We have found that the whole number is 128, because 64 will divide 128 times, into 8195 with a small remainder (0.0468). When we multiply this remainder times the denominator, we obtain 2.9952. When rounded off to 3, this number represents the numerator of the mixed fraction. Note that if we had a large calculator, our answer would be 3, but since we are limited with many of the present-day personal calculators to 8 digits, exact figures cannot always be obtained. Our final answer, expressed as a mixed fraction, is $128 \, 3/64$

Multiplying Mixed Fractions Word Problem

What is the cost of 2¾ tons of coal at $20.50 a ton? Convert both mixed numbers to decimal form and multiply.

Procedure

Operation	Keyboard Entry	Function Touch	Display	Description
Set decimal to three places				
Clear registers and display		C	0.000	
Enter number of tons in decimal form	2.75	x	2.750	
Enter cost per ton	20.5	=	56.375	Answer

The coal will cost $56.38.

DIVIDING FRACTIONS

The procedure for dividing fractions is a little different than almost any other type of mathematical operation, but the procedure is simple to master.

Solve the following problem.

$$1/3 \div 7/8 = ?$$

To divide one fraction by another, we simply invert the fraction of the divisor, and multiply the fraction thus obtained by the dividend. You will recall that the number to be divided in a problem is called the dividend, and the number we are dividing by is called the divisor. The above problem, stated in words, is to divide ⅓ by ⅞. Therefore, ⅓ is the dividend, and ⅞ the divisor. If we invert the fraction of the divisor, we have ⁸⁄₇, and the problem can be restated as

$$1/3 \times 8/7 = ?$$

Now, the problem appears as a multiplication problem, similar to the previous two problems.

Procedure

Operation	Keyboard Entry	Function Touch	Display	Description
Set decimal to zero places				
Clear registers and display		C	0	
Enter numerator of 1/3	1	x	1	
Enter numerator of 8/7	8	=	8	Numerator of answer (record)
Clear registers and display		C	0	

Operation	Keyboard Entry	Function Touch	Display	Description
Enter denominator of 1 / 3	3	x	3	
Enter denominator of 8 / 7	7	=	21	Denominator of answer

The answer is 8 / 21.

Dividing Mixed Fractions

What is 6⅞ divided by 3 ⅐ ?

We must first convert the mixed fractions to improper fractions, invert the improper fraction of the divisor, and multiply the fraction thus obtained by the dividend.

Procedure

Operation	Keyboard Entry	Function Touch	Display	Description
Set decimal to zero places				
Clear registers and display		C	0	
Enter denominator of dividend	8	x	8	
Enter whole numer of dividend	6		48	
Transfer display to add register	None	+	48	
Add numerator of dividend	7		55	Numerator of improper fraction, or divisor (record)
Clear registers and display		C	0	
Enter denominator of divisor	7	x	7	
Enter whole number of divisor	2		21	
Transfer display to add register	None	+	21	
Add numerator of divisor	1		22	

The problem can now be stated as follows:

$$55 / 8 \div 22 / 7 = ?$$

By inverting the fraction of the divisor, and multiplying the inverted fraction by the dividend, the problem can be restated as

$$55 / 8 \times 7 / 22 = ?$$

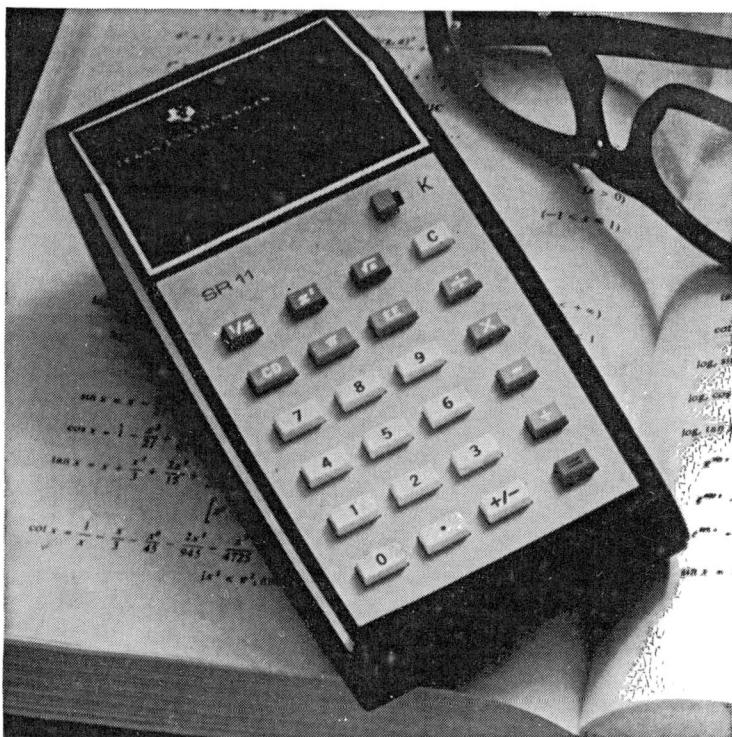

TEXAS INSTRUMENTS MODEL SR-11—The manufacturer refers to its SR-11 as an **electronic slide rule.** The 12-character display (8-digit mantissa, 2 signs, 2-digit exponent) is of the light-emitting-diode type, which shows all numerals, floating decimal, negative signs, calculation overflow, and error indication, plus a low-battery warning. The calculator will display positive and negative numbers as large as 99999999×10^{99} and as small as $1.0000000 \times 10^{-98}$. It is designed to replace the classical slide rule.

The keyboard consists of 10 digit keys plus decimal point, 12 function keys, the K switch, and **pi** key. All keys are single function for simple problem entry. In addition to the standard four functions of addition, subtraction, multiplication, and division, the SR-11 calculation capabilities include reciprocals, squares, square root, change of sign, scientific notation, automatic conversion to scientific notation when 8-digit mantissa overflows, and mixed calculations. Data may be entered in free form—that is, floating decimal point, scientific notation, or any combination of the two.

The SR-11 electronic calculator contains 3 ni-cad, fast-charge batteries (standard AA size) that provide 4-6 hours of continuous use before recharging is required. The ac adapter/charger (included) will recharge the batteries from normal house current in about 3 hours. The SR-11 automatically turns off the display, except for the character in the far-right digit position of the mantissa, approximately 15 to 60 seconds after the last key is pressed. This standby mode conserves battery power during nonuse periods. The results of the calculation will be restored to the display when the + key is pressed twice. **Texas Instruments, Dallas, Texas 75222.**

The problem is now solved in the same manner as a multiplication problem.

Procedure

Operation	Keyboard Entry	Function Touch	Display	Description
Clear registers and display		C	0	
Enter numerator of 55 ∕ 8	55	x	55	
Enter numerator of 7 ∕ 22	7	=	385	Numerator of answer (record)
Clear registers and display		C	0	
Enter denominator of 55 ∕ 8	8	x	8	
Enter denominator of 7 ∕ 22	22	=	176	Denominator of answer (record)

The answer, expressed as an improper fraction, is $385 / 176$. This must be converted to a mixed fraction.

Procedure

Operation	Keyboard Entry	Function Touch	Display	Description
Clear registers and display				
Set decimal to five places		C	0	
Enter numerator of answer expressed as improper fraction	385	÷	385	
Enter denominator of answer	176	=	2.18750	Answer expressed as a decimal (record)
Clear registers and display		C	0.00000	
Enter decimal part of answer just obtained	.1875	x	0.18750	
Enter denominator	176	≡	33.00000	Numerator of fraction

We have found that 2 is the whole number of the answer $(385 / 176 = 2.18750)$, and that the fraction 0.18750, when multiplied by the denominator, 176, equals 33. Therefore, our answer, expressed as a mixed fraction, is $2\,{}^{33}/_{176}$. By experimentation, we find that the answer reduces to $2\,{}^{3}/_{16}$

Dividing Mixed Fractions Word Problem

How many rods $6\frac{1}{3}$ in. long can be cut from a 12 ft length of wirebar?

The first step in this problem is to convert the length of the wirebar from feet to inches. We must then divide the total length of the wirebar by the length of each rod. Since $6\frac{1}{3}$ is a mixed fraction, it must be converted to an improper fraction to perform the calculations.

Procedure

Operation	Keyboard Entry	Function Touch	Display	Description
Set decimal to two places				
Clear registers and display		C	0.00	
Enter number of feet in wirebar	12	x	12.00	
Enter number of inches in a foot	12	=	144.00	Length of wirebar in inches (record)
Clear registers and display		C	0.00	
Enter denominator of 1 / 3	3	x	3.00	First step in converting mixed fraction to
Enter whole number of length of rod (6-1 / 3 in.)	6	=	18.00	improper fraction
Transfer display to add register	None	+	18.00	
Enter numerator of 1 / 3	1	=	19.00	Numerator of improper fraction (denominator remains unchanged)

We have now determined that the mixed fraction 6⅓, when converted to an improper fraction, is 19 / 3. Remember that 144 is the dividend, and 19 / 3 is the divisor. The problem can now be restated as

$$144/1 \div 19/3 = 144/1 \text{ x } 3/19 = ?$$

The final solution follows.

Operation	Keyboard Entry	Function Touch	Display	Description
Clear registers and display		C	0.00	
Enter numerator of first fraction	144	x	144.00	
Enter numerator of second fraction	3	=	432.00	Numerator of answer (improper fraction) (record)
Clear registers and display		C	0.00	
Enter denominator of first fraction	1	x	1.00	
Enter denominator of second fraction	19	=	19.00	Denominator of answer (record)
Clear registers and display		C	0.00	
Enter numerator from improper fraction just determined above	432	÷	432.00	To convert to proper fraction
Enter denominator of answer	19	=	22.73	Answer in decimal form

Since the problem asks how many rods can be cut, we are not concerned with fractional parts of rods. Therefore, we see that we can cut 22 rods each 6⅓ in. long from a 12 ft wirebar. We will have a short piece left over.

MULTIPLE MATHEMATICAL OPERATIONS

This section contains several problems in which more than one of the basic mathematical functions are employed. These exercises are word problems, which, when broken down into parts, become easy to solve on the electronic calculator.

Multiplying and Dividing Fractions

If 6⅞ tons of coal cost $96.25 what is the cost of 11⅓ tons?

Calculate the cost of a ton of coal, and then multiply that cost times 11⅓. Convert all mixed numbers to decimal form prior to attacking the problem.

Procedure

Operation	Keyboard Entry	Function Touch	Display	Description
Set decimal to four places				
Clear registers and display		C	0.0000	
Enter numerator of 7 / 8	7	÷	7.0000	
Enter denominator of 7 / 8	8		0.8750	Fractional form of 7/ 8 (record)
Clear registers and display		C	0.0000	
Enter numerator of 1 / 3	1	÷	1.0000	
Enter denominator of 1 / 3	3	=	0.3333	Fractional form of 1/ 3 (record)
Clear registers and display		C	0.0000	
Enter cost of 6 7 / 8 tons of coal	96.25	÷	96.2500	
Enter 6 7 / 8 in decimal form	6.875	=	14.0000	Cost per ton
Transfer display to multiply register	None	x	14.0000	
Enter 11-1 / 3 tons in decimal form	11.3333	=	158.6662	Answer

The cost of 11⅓ tons of coal
That was easy, wasn't it? But the next problem is a little harder—it requires a little analysis.

Time Distribution

A certain airliner left a remote airport with 170 persons aboard. It crashed an hour later in a desolate section of the

110

world, with only nine survivors. Fortunately, none of the supplies were damaged. Ordinarily, these supplies would sustain 170 people for 3 weeks. How long will the supplies last the survivors?

Of the total supplies, one person will use 1/170 in 3 weeks. We can divide 1/170 by 3 to find a week's supply for one person, and multiply the product by 9 to determine a week's supply for nine persons. Once we have found the weekly consumption, we can divide that amount into the whole to find the number of weeks the supplies will last. We will let the number 1 represent all of the supplies.

The first part of the problem is stated as follows:

$$1/170 \div 3/1 = ?$$

Remember that we can place a 1 under any number without changing its value, and in this case, we have placed a 1 under the 3. As explained in previous problems, to divide one fraction by another, we invert the fraction of the divisor (3/1) and multiply the fraction thus obtained (1/3) by the dividend. The first part of the problem is restated as

$$1/170 \quad x \quad 1/3 = ?$$

Procedure

Operation	Keyboard Entry	Function Touch	Display	Description
Set decimal to zero places				
Clear registers and display		C	0	
Enter denominator of 1 / 170	170	x	170	
Enter denominator of 1 / 3	3	=	510	Denominator of first part of problem

We know that

$$1 x 1 = 1$$

Hence we have determined that one person will consume 1/510 of the supplies per week. Therefore, nine people will consume 9/510 of the supplies per week. If 9/510 of the supplies are consumed weekly, how long will it take to consume all of the supplies? Restated, how many times can 1/1 (the whole) be divided by 9/510?

$$1/1 \div 9/510 = 1/1 \ x \ 510/9 = 510/9 = ?$$

We see that we must now simply divide 510 by 9.

Procedure

Operation	Keyboard Entry	Function Touch	Display	Description
Set decimal to five places				Three digits must be used for the number 510, leaving 5 digits for the decimal, if there is a decimal.
Clear registers and display		C	0.00000	
Enter 510	510	÷	500.00000	
Enter 9	9	=	56.66666	Answer (in weeks)

The supplies will last 56 ⅔ weeks—slightly over a year.

Labor Distribution

The next exercise is a typical problem in labor distribution, but it is written in everyday terms. Scheduling and production in large factories are activities where problems of this nature must be solved.

Time Distribution

If 6 bricklayers can build a wall in 8 hours, how long will it take 11 bricklayers to build the same wall?

The solution to any time distribution problem is usually started by breaking down the problem into single units, if possible. In this problem we must first determine how much of the wall one bricklayer can built in 1h. We then multiply that figure by the number of bricklayers (11) to give us the fraction the wall one bricklayer can build in 1 hour. We then multiply that figure by the number of bricklayers (11) to give us the fraction of the wall that will be built in 1 hour. We know that the fraction represents the whole (100 percent) of the wall, so we simply divide by the fraction of the wall that 11 men will do in 1 hour, and we will arrive at the answer.

In 1 hour, ⅛ of the wall is done by six bricklayers. Therefore, one bricklayer will lay of ⅛ of the wall in an hour.

Procedure

Operation	Keyboard Entry	Function Touch	Display	Description
Set decimal to three places				
Clear registers and display		C	0.000	
Enter denominator of 1 / 6	6	x	6.000	
Enter denominator of 1 / 8	8	=	48.000	

We see that

$$1/6 \times 1/8 = 1/48$$

This is the portion of the wall that one bricklayer can build in 1hr The next step in solving the problem is to multiply the number of bricklayers times what one bricklayer can do in 1h. We will then know what fraction of the wall 11 bricklayers can do in 1hr. This is a step we can do without the use of the electronic calculator.

$$11 \times 1/48 = 11/48$$

We find that $11/48$ of the wall can be built by 11 bricklayers in 1hr. To find how many hours it will take the 11 bricklayers to do the whole wall, we must divide the whole, $1/1$ by $11/48$

$$1/1 \div 11/48 = 1/1 \times 48/_{11} = 48/11 \, hr$$

Procedure

Operation	Keyboard Entry	Function Touch	Display	Description
Clear registers and display		C	0.000	
Enter numerator of improper fraction just determined	48	÷	48.000	
Enter denominator of improper fraction just determined	11	=	4.363	Answer

It will take 11 bricklayers 4.363 hr to build the same wall that 6 bricklayers could build in 8 hr.

Using algebra, this problem would be solved somewhat differently. An equation would be developed, with **a** as the unknown:

6 bricklayers times 8 hours equals 11 bricklayers times ? hours

or

$$6 \times 8 = 11 \times a$$

Dividing both sides of the equation by 11

$$\frac{6 \times 8}{11} = a$$

113

The unknown, a, is now isolated to one side of the equation. Doing the multiplication, we have

$$48/11 = a$$

This equation is solved on the electronic calculator as above. We see that the use of algebra can sometimes make problem solving much easier.

Unit Pricing

Unit pricing for the consumer is the process of determining what the same units of measure of two or more competitive products will cost, to enable him to make the best buy. The products under consideration must be equal or nearly equal in quality.

Quality vs Quantity

In discussing unit pricing, we must understand what factors have real meaning in comparing competitive products. For instance, one market may offer T-bone steaks at a price of $2.89 a pound, while another market offers T-bone steaks at $3.50 a pound. Are these steaks of identical quality? By shopping at both markets, you may have realized that the $3.50 steak has superior taste, and perhaps you would rather pay extra for the better tasting steak.

Neither weight nor taste is going to tell us how much nutrition we're going to get out of a dollar spent for T-bone steak at either market. The closest we can come to making a valid nutritional comparison is to note the U.S. Department of Agriculture (USDA) grades on these steaks. If they are the same grade, then we must assume that they offer approximately the same nutritional value per pound. If the steaks are not the same grade, we can make inquiry to the Department of Agriculture for information relative to the comparative nutritional values per pound between the two grades, and from that information, decide if the difference is important to us. However, if the steaks are of the same grade, and the taste and texture are almost equal, we will, of course, buy the $2.89 steak.

Papers and Weights

When we are buying writing paper, we are not much concerned with the price per pound. In this case, we must look at the price per unit **area**, even though weight is an important consideration to the manufacturer and to large buyers of paper. When we're at the stationery store and we are presented with a choice of two different brands of typing paper—substantially the same in quality—then we will be comparing price per sheet, per 100 sheets, or per 500 sheets.

With paper towels that we use in the kitchen, on the other hand, we are generally very much concerned with both the area and the thickness. The product of the area and the thickness gives **volume**. Since a large number of brands are approximately the same density, this means that the meaningful units of measure for paper towels will be volume and weight. This is not the what we found for writing paper.

Fortunately, most products are sold by weight or volume, and this information is marked on the package. If ingredients are fully and quantitatively stated (they usually are not, even in health food stores) and happen to be identical among competitive products, then it will be safe to assume that the quality is about the same. Otherwise, this assumption would not be valid. If the pressure of competition in the marketplace forces competing manufacturers, growers, and packagers to cut the quality of their products equally to the point where the lack of quality becomes apparent, then we may assume that the quality of competing products is roughly equal. But we must look carefully at the equality as far as the purchase price is concerned. If we assume that the quality is about the same, then it becomes meaningful to compare prices of products of the same general kind. Our unit of measurement may be dollars per pound, cents per pound, cents per ounce, or whatever. With our comparisons accomplished—unit to unit—we then apply our common sense and purchase the best buy for the money.

Liquids

Liquids such as gasoline, orange juice, and milk can be compared on either a weight basis (ounces or pounds) or on a volume basis (fluid ounces or quarts); because liquids are incompressible, they do not change density with time or packaging conditions. The octane of the gasoline you buy should be matched to the engine of your automobile, and this oftentimes depends upon the engine's timing. Aside from that, it is wise to buy the cheapest gasoline you can get per gallon, since they are all equally corrosive and since the chemical constituents (over 3000 of them) in gasoline have never been completely analyzed by any billion-dollar oil company (or even by any billion-dollar government agency). They're not

SUMMIT MODEL SE88M—The manufacturer of this little gem claims the SE88M replaces the conventional slide rule by offering greater speed and accuracy, plus a memory system. Besides giving 8-place accuracy in all functions, it will directly solve square root, square, reciprocal, and percentage problems. With one hand, you can hold and operate all 8 functions and the memory of the SE88M. Algebraic logic lets you solve problems the same way you would write them, and direct negative entry and negative readout permit operations involving mixed signs to achieve results with the correct sign. The decimal system assures that your answers will always be decimally correct, with your choice of full floating decimal, or a selection of fixed places from 0 to 7. The results on the brightly lit display will be rounded off to the nearest number.

The instrument features an 8-digit display, but it will calculate internally with up to 16 digits. If the result is more than 8 digits, the keyboard locks to prevent errors, and an overflow system appears in the display until the keyboard is cleared. Built-in ni-cad batteries recharge in just 3 hours to give 10 full hours of operating time, and the readout automatically goes out after holding the same number for 15 seconds to conserve battery power. A tiny symbol appears to indicate that the calculator is still on, and it is possible to recall the last number simply by pressing the M key.

The unit weighs only 8¼ ounces and measures 2¾ x 4 x 1⅛ inches. Each calculator is delivered with an ac charger and a deluxe padded carrying pouch. It has a one-year warranty. **Summit International Corporation, 180 West 2950 South, Salt Lake City, Utah 84115.**

trying to gyp you...they don't even know what they're selling you.

Large Economy Size

If we were to take the time to compare the large economy size with the regular size, we would find that in many cases the large economy size actually costs **more** per unit than the regular size! In the sample problems given in this chapter, we have used actual prices found in some of the large markets, and changed the brand names. In one market, a certain brand of toothpaste costs noticeably more if the large economy size is purchased instead of the regular size. In the same market, several other economy sizes cost more per unit than did the regular or smaller sizes. This method of pricing is found in other markets as well.

BASIC UNIT-PRICING CALCULATIONS

The unit price is obtained by dividing cost by the number of units purchased. For example, if a 46 oz can of pineapple juice costs 38 cents, each ounce (our unit of measurement) will cost 38 cents divided by 46 oz, or 0.826 cent per ounce. It may be more convenient for us to express the unit cost in quarts, rather than ounces, in which case we must multiply the cost per ounce by 32 (ounces per quart) to obtain a figure of 26.435 cents per quart.

In some places in the United States, it is mandatory that the grocery markets post unit prices for the consumers to review at the time of purchase. But a close look often tells us that the unit prices are not updated with price changes. Therefore, it is wise to calculate the unit prices yourself with the help of the electronic calculator. You have the added advantage of expressing the prices in any unit you desire, rather than in only the unit price posted. Posting of unit prices is indeed helpful, but it is not mandatory in most localities. It is an expense to the markets to post unit prices, and therefore, to enable them to compete successfully, this is a frill that is not normally found unless required by law.

Unit-Pricing Formulas

Basically, the most important thing to remember in calculating unit prices for comparison purposes is to divide the cost by the unit of measure. If five grapefruits cost 49 cents in one market, and three grapefruits cost 29 cents in another market, we can find the cost per grapefruit by dividing the cost by the number received. A more accurate method might be to weigh the grapefruits, and then to calculate a cost per pound, but this method would not be practical if the two markets were across town from each other. Within a market, two different situations like this could exist, where comparison by weight unit cost would be feasible; but it certainly would not be economical to drive from one market to another to save a tenth of a cent per grapefruit!

Suppose an item cost $3 per pound, and we wanted to compare it with the same item that was priced at $1.95 for 11 oz. We can easily convert the 11 oz measurement to its cost per pound by referring to Table I. In the column marked **Unit price desired**, we find **Dollars per pound**. The second product above is measured in ounces, and priced in dollars. The table tells us that the method to be used is: Multiply 16 times price divided by weight. The price is $1.95 (in dollars) and the weight is 11 (in ounces). If we carry out the indicated calculation, we have $2.83632 as the cost per pound. Clearly, the 11 oz package—at $3 per pound—is a better buy.

How to Use Table I

Refer to the package and notice how the product is priced (in cents or in dollars), and how the package contents are measured (ounces, pounds, pints, etc.) Determine the unit-price category desired, whether it is cents per ounce, dollars per pound, cents per quart, or whatever, and read down the **Unit price desired** column to that section. On one line in that section, you will find the combination of weight and price that is on the package, and the method to be used to arrive at the unit price desired.

For example, if dollars per pound is the unit price desired, and the package is measured in ounces and priced in cents, read down the **Unit price desired** column to the **Dollars per pound** section. Within that section, under the **Product measured in** and **Product priced in** columns, you will find a line with both **ounces** and **cents**. Read across on this line to the **method** column, which states, "Multiply 0.16 times price divided by weight.

If the product is priced in cents, do not enter a decimal point to indicate a fraction of a dollar. The cents are to be entered as a whole number. If a decimal point were to be entered in the calculator, we would be entering **dollars** (or fractions of dollars) instead of cents. The readout on the display will be in dollars, calculated automatically, if the proper method is followed and dollars are desired as the unit price. If the unit price is desired in cents, the whole numbers on the display will be in cents.

Table I. Obtaining Unit Prices.

Unit price desired	Product measured in	Product priced in	Method
Cents per ounce	Ounces	Cents	Divide price by weight
	Ounces	Dollars	Multiply 100 times price divided by weight
	Pounds	Cents	Divide price by weight, divide quotient by 16 (ounces per pound)
	Pounds	Dollars	Multiply 6.25 times price divided by weight
Cents per fluid ounce	Fl ounces	Cents	Divide price by volume
	Gallon	Dollars	Multiply 0.7812 times price divided by volume
	Quarts	Dollars	Multiply 3.125 times price divided by volume
	Gallon	Cents	Multiply 0.007812 times price divided by volume
	Quarts	Dollars	Multiply 0.03125 times price divided by volume
	Pints	Cents	Multiply 0.0625 times price divided by volume
Dollars per pound	Pounds	Dollars	Divide price by weight
	Pounds	Cents	Divide price by weight, divide quotient by 100
	Ounces	Dollars	Multiply 16 times price divided by weight
	Ounces	Cents	Multiply 0.16 times price divided by weight
Dollars per ounce	Ounces	Dollars	Divide price by weight
Cents per pint	Pints	Cents	Divide price by volume
	Quarts	Dollars	Multiply 50 times price divided by volume
	Fl ounces	Cents	Multiply 16 times price divided by volume
Cents per pint	Quarts	Cents	Multiply 0.5 times price divided by volume
	Gallons	Cents	Multiply 0.125 times price divided by volume
	Gallons	Dollars	Multiply 12.5 times price divided by volume
Cents per quart	Quarts	Cents	Divide price by volume
	Fl ounces	Cents	Multiply 32 times price divided by volume
	Pint	Cents	Multiply 2 times price divided by volume
	Quarts	Dollars	Multiply 100 times price divided by volume
	Gallons	Cents	Multiply 0.25 times price divided by volume
Dollars per quart	Quarts	Dollars	Divide price by volume
	Gallons	Dollars	Multiply 25 times price divided by volume
Cents per gallon	Gallons	Cents	Divide price by volume
Dollars per gallon	Gallons	Dollars	Divide price by volume
	Fl ounces	Cents	Multiply 1.28 times price divided by volume
	Pints	Cents	Multiply 0.08 times price divided by volume
	Quarts	Cents	Multiply 0.04 times price divided by volume
	Quarts	Dollars	Multiply 4 times price divided by volume
	Gallons	Cents	Divide price by volume, divide quotient by 100

UNIT-PRICING EXERCISES

The exercises in this chapter are typical problems that may confront the shopper when he arrives at the supermarket. Master this section before your next shopping trip. When you return home, sit down and figure out how much you saved by checking out unit prices before you bought. It may be surprising!

Economy Size Toothpaste

A supermarket carries a regular size tube of toothpaste, net weight 6¾ oz, for 66 cents, and an economy size tube of the same brand, net weight 8¾ oz, for 86 cents. The sales tax where the market is located is 5 percent on nonfood items. How much of a saving per ounce does one gain by buying the economy size? (Note: 5 percent is 0.05, when expressed as a decimal.)

Procedure

Operation	Keyboard Entry	Function Touch	Display	Description
Set decimal to three places				
Clear registers and display		C	0.000	
Enter price factor	66	x	66.000	Price of regular tube
Enter tax factor (1 plus tax rate as a decimal)	1.05	=	69.300	Regular price including tax
Transfer display to dividend register	None	÷	69.300	
Enter divisor (regular weight)	6.75	=	10.266	Cost per ounce in regular tube (record)
Clear registers and display		C	0.000	
Enter price factor	86	x	86.000	Price of economy tube
Enter tax factor	1.05	=	90.300	Economy pric including tax
Transfer display to dividend register	None	÷	90.300	
Enter divisor (economy weight)	8.75	=	10.320	Cost per ounce in economy tube

Note that after rounding, the cost of the regular tube is 10.27 cents per ounce, which is less than the 10.32 cents per ounce in the alleged economy tube. There is no saving per ounce in buying the economy size in this case.

Sunflower Seeds by the Ounce and Pound

Market A and Market B sell a 4½ oz package of sunflower seeds for 29 cents. Market A has 1 lb bags of sunflower seeds on sale at 89 cents. Market B has 1 lb 6 oz bags of sunflower seeds on sale at $1.11 each. Which sunflower seeds are the best buy?

Procedure

Operation	Keyboard Entry	Function Touch	Display	Description
Set decimal to three places				
Clear registers and display		C	0.000	
Enter price factor	29	÷	29.000	Price of 4½ oz package
Enter divisor (weight)	4.5	=	6.444	Cost per ounce in 4½ oz package (record)
Clear registers and display		C	0.000	
Enter price factor	89	÷	89.00	Price of pound bag
Enter divisor (weight converted to ounces)	16	=	5.562	Cost per ounce in pound package (record)
Clear registers and display		C	0.000	
Enter price factor (converted to cents)	111	÷	111.000	Price of 1 lb 6½ oz bag
Enter divisor (weight converted to ounces)	22.5	=	4.933	Cost per ounce in Market B's 1 lb 6½ oz bag.

The three rounded costs—6.44 cents per ounce, 5.56 cents per ounce, and 4.93 cents per ounce—show that Market B wins hands down with their 1 lb 6 oz bag at $1.11.

Juices and Drinks by the Quart, Ounce, Pint, and Milliliter

All juices and drinks are mostly water and have a density about equal to that of water. Therefore, one can buy them either by volume or by weight after making cost comparisons. Suppose that I have decided to ferret out the cheapest juice regardless of kind, and to buy it. Suppose also that I find apple juice at 56 cents for 32 fl oz, concentrated orange juice (frozen, and requiring mixture with three cans of cold water) at 56 cents for a 6½ fl oz can, grapefruit juice at 43 cents a quart, and pineapple juice at 23 cents a pint. Which shall I buy?

Procedure

Operation	Keyboard Entry	Function Touch	Display	Description
Set decimal to three places				
Clear registers and display		C	0.000	
Enter apple price	56	÷	56.000	

Operation	Keyboard Entry	Function Touch	Display	Description
Enter apple volume (all volumes in fluid ounces	32	=	1.750	Apple cost, cents per ounce (record)
Clear registers and display		C	0.000	
Enter equivalent cans of reconstituted orange juice (1 + 3)	4	x	4.000	
Enter volume of one can	6.5	=	26.000	Volume of reconstituted orange juice (record)
Clear registers and display		C	0.000	
Enter orange price	56	÷	56.000	
Enter orange volume	26	=	2.153	Orange cost, cents per ounce (record)
Clear registers and display		C	0.000	
Enter grapefruit price	43	÷	43.000	
Enter grapefruit volume (converted to fluid ounces)	32	=	1.343	Grapefruit cost, cents per ounce (record)
Clear registers and display		C	0.000	
Enter pineapple price	23	÷	23.000	
Enter pineapple volume (converted to fluid ounces)	16	=	1.437	Pinapple cost, cents per ounce (record)
Clear registers and display				

Our recorded answers should now look something like this:

Apple juice	1.75 cents per fluid ounce
Orange juice	2.15 cents per fluid ounce
Grapefruit juice	1.34 cents per fluid ounce
Pineapple juice	1.44 cents per fluid ounce

Clearly, grapefruit juice is the lowest priced, and that is what I should buy.

ENGLISH* AND METRIC PRICING SYSTEMS

We have included in this chapter a few exercises involving price conversions from metric to English, so that you may compare the two systems and be exposed to conversion techniques. You will find the electronic calculator very helpful if you are ever required to compare metric and English prices.

---

*The system in current use in the U.S. is called officially the **English** system. Interestingly, the English use another, called the **British** system.

TOSHIBA MODEL BC-1204—The Toshiba BC-1204 is a 12-digit electronic desk calculator designed to minimize the workload. It capably performs ordinary business calculations such as constant and discount operations, as well as the four fundamental arithmetic operations. It features easy-to-read multidigit display tubes developed by Toshiba and a size that is ideal for desktop duty.

Up to 12 digits, the most-significant-digit system takes over, and the upper-digit figures from the top are given priority sequentially. However, if the integral part exceeds 12 digits, the calculator overflows. Eyestrain is relieved, even after long-hour use, by Toshiba's bright, large multidigit tube developed recently by the manufacturer. The constant is automatically locked, facilitating multiply-divide operations merely by setting the constant switch. The figures fed and the intermediate results are shown by a floating decimal point, while the result is displayed at a preset decimal point. The result is also shown at the floating decimal point, ideally suited for obtaining exact answers at any time desired. Roundoff is possible in all four fundamental arithmetic operations by actuating the roundoff switch, and the zero suppression system prohibits indication of unwanted zeros. The unit features a 12-digit 3-register underflow system, an exchange key for swapping dividend and divisor in division calculations (including reciprocal calculations), and an automatic percentage or discount functions, in a lightweight, portable size. The unit measures about 6½ x 2½ x 9½ inches, and weighs less than 2¼ pounds. **Toshiba America, Inc., 41-06 Delong Street, Flushing, N.Y. 11355.**

Unit Pricing between English and Metric Volumes

At Six Continents Health Food Store, Mrs. Jackson finds papaya juice from the same New Caledonia cannery with two different forms of pricing. Some cans are marked 1.4 liters and sell for 80 cents. Other are marked 46 fl oz and sell for 75 cents. Which cans will be more economical for Mrs. Jackson to buy?

To convert liters to fluid ounces, we must multiply the liters by 33.8150 to obtain fluid ounces.

Procedure

Operation	Keyboard Entry	Function Touch	Display	Description
Set decimal to four places				
Clear registers and display		C	0.0000	
Enter conversion factor (liters to fluid ounces)	33.8150	x	33.8150	
Enter metric quantity	1.4	=	47.3410	First quantity, fluid ounces (record)
Clear registers and display		C	0.0000	
Enter metric price	80	÷	80.0000	
Enter first quantity	47.341	=	1.6899	Metric unit price, cents per fluid ounce (record)
Clear registers and display		C	0.0000	
Enter English price	75	÷	75.0000	
Enter English quantity	46	=	1.6304	English unit price (cents per fluid ounce)

Comparing unit prices, we see that the 46 fl oz cans will be more economical for Mrs. Jackson to buy.

Unit Pricing between English and Metric Weights

At Seven Seas Fish Market, Mrs. Van Buren finds imported tinned sardines with two different forms of pricing. Some cans are marked 400 grams and sell for 82 cents. Others are marked 15 oz and sell for $1. Which cans will be more economical for Mrs. Van Buren to buy?

To convert grams to ounces, we must multiply the grams by 0.0353.

Procedure

Operation	Keyboard Entry	Function Touch	Display	Description
Set decimal to four places				
Clear registers and display		C	0.0000	

Operation	Keyboard Entry	Function Touch	Display	Description
Enter conversion factor (grams to ounces)	0.0353	x	0.0353	
Enter metric quantity	400	=	14.1200	Converted quantity, ounces (record)
Clear registers and display		C	0.0000	
Enter metric price	82	÷	82.0000	
Enter converted quantity	14.12	=	5.8074	Metric unit price, cents per ounce (record)
Clear registers and display		C	0.0000	
Enter English price	100	÷	100.0000	
Enter English quantity	15	=	6.6667	English unit price, cents per ounce

Comparing unit prices, we see that the 400g tins will be more economical for Mrs. Van Buren to buy.

Comparing Kilograms and Pounds

Mrs. Harrison finds Danish hams at $3.15 per kilogram and Australian hams at $1.50 a pound. Which are more economical for her to buy, assuming equal quality and flavor?

To convert kilograms to pounds, we must divide the kilograms by 2.2046.

Procedure

Operation	Keyboard Entry	Function Touch	Display	Description
Set decimal to four places				
Clear registers and display		C	0.0000	
Enter price of metric-priced ham	3.15	÷	3.1500	
Enter conversion factor (pounds in a kilogram)	2.2046	=	1.4288	Price per pound of Danish hams

The Danish hams at $1.43 per pound are more economical for Mrs. Harrison to buy.

Comparing Gallons and Liters

Mrs. Tyler finds Sask brand homogenized milk advertised at 56 cents per half-gallon and at 28 cents per liter in two adjacent stores in Bordertown. Which milk is more economical for Mrs. Tyler to buy?

We will first convert the half-gallon of milk to cost per gallon. Next, using the conversion factor of 0.2642, we will

TEXAS INSTRUMENTS MODEL TI-2510—The TI-2510 keyboard consists of 10 digit keys, a decimal key, and 7 function keys, with each key having a soft but positive touch. All keys are single-function, allowing simple entry of long or complex mathematical problems. The user just presses the keys exactly as the problem is stated. Easy to read and operate, the keys are located for maximum performance, and by using the raised dot on key 5 for reference, complex problems can be performed without looking at the keyboard. A chain-constant switch located on the keyboard selects either the **constant** mode (for convenient multiplication or division by a constant number) or the **chain** mode (for normal calculations).

The 8-digit light-emitting-diode readout is clearly visible from either hand-held or desktop operation. The readout shows all numerals, floating decimal, negative sign, calculation overflow indication, and entry overflow indication. The bright appearance of the display will not tire the user's eyes even after long periods of operation. Power is supplied to the unit by 4 replaceable alkaline batteries that deliver the equivalent of 15 hours of continuous calculation before replacement. Or the optional ac adapter allows use of the standard household outlets.

In addition to the four basic mathematical functions, the TI-2510 handles credit balances, chain multiplication and division, constant multiplication and division, and it employs a full floating decimal system. It measures 5½ x 3 x 1¾ inches, and weighs 10 ounces. **Texas Instruments, Inc., Dallas, Texas 75222.**

multiply the price of 1 liter of milk by the factor to arrive at a cost per gallon, and compare the two prices.

Procedure

Operation	Keyboard Entry	Function Touch	Display	Description
Set decimal to four places				
Clear registers and display		C	0.0000	
Enter English price	0.56	÷	0.5600	
Enter English volume	0.5	=	1.1200	English unit price per gallon (record)
Clear registers and display		C	0.0000	
Enter metric price	0.28	÷	0.2800	
Enter conversion factor (gallons in a liter)	0.2642	=	1.0598	Metric unit price per gallon

Mrs. Tyler will find it more economical to buy her milk at the store selling it for 28 cents per liter.

Grocery Shopping

Grocery shopping with the electronic calculator can be an experience. When the realization hits that you have been paying too much for your family's food bills over the years, it is a depressing experience. But to know that starting now you will be shopping wisely is a pleasant experience! It is estimated that each year the average family spends approximately $75 to $100 more than is necessary, through unwise shopping practices. It is not that the average shopper is foolish. There are a number of factors that contribute to this waste of his earnings. Let's look at a few.

CHECKOUT ERRORS

In many large supermarkets, the customer fills his shopping cart and rolls it up to the checkout counter. The counter is arranged so that the checker is operating the cash register at the same time the customer is unloading the cart. This keeps the shopper from checking the prices being rung up on the register. Suppose the checker makes a mistake and rings up an overcharge. It may well go unnoticed by both the shopper and the checker.

How do you keep this from happening? Probably the best bet is to shop with another person; while one is unloading the shopping cart, the other can keep an eagle eye on the register. Sometimes, that's impractical. You might unload the cart as fast as you could, and then race around to where you could carefully watch, hoping that the checker hasn't made too many mistakes on the items already rung up before you got the cart completely unloaded. As an alternative, you might try to find a market where the clerk unloaded the cart, thereby giving you the opportunity to observe the cash register as each item passes through.

Not only are checkout clerks under pressure to check out the customers as fast as possible to please the store manager, checkers must also work fast to please the customers. The old saying that haste makes waste has a definite application here. The waste, however, comes out of the family food budget.

TOSHIBA MODEL BC-0804B—Toshiba's **instant genius** is their new model BC-0804B electronic calculator, which operates from household power or its own integral dry batteries, or with an optional rechargeable ni-cad battery. The unit will handle all four fundamental arithmetical operations with or without roundoff, chain multiplication and division, mixed calculation, constant calculations, and other applied operations. Add-on calculations are simply performed by pressing a specific key twice; discount calculations are handled by pressing the minus key and the plus-equal key in succession. The clearly legible display tubes operate on a zero suppression system; that is, all zeros above the first figures are not displayed, and the minus indicator is illuminated when the result of the calculation is a negative number.

The calculator handles virtually all normal calculations in offices, stores, scores of other businesses, and in general home use. In multiplication or division, 8 digits times 8 digits, or 8 digits divided by 8 digits is feasible, the most significant 8 digits from the top displayed on the indicator. The constant switch can be activated to calculate multiplication or division with a constant factor. The instrument has a choice of either the floating or fixed decimal point system merely by setting the decimal switch. In the designated mode, the decimal point can be set either at 0 or 2 decimal digits. When the decimal point is set at either 0 or 2, all calculations come under the roundoff function, while no roundoff is effected with the floating decimal point. An indicator tells when replacement of the batteries is required. The unit measures 4⅛ x 1⅝ x 6⅞ inches, and weighs 1⅛ pounds. **Toshiba America, Inc., 41-06 Delong Street, Flushing, New York 11355.**

I don't want to give the impression that it is the policy of the markets to purposely overcharge their customers. I have never heard of any market with a policy such as that. On the contrary, the prices legitimately charged by the markets take into account the clerk's salary, shoplifting, and all the other expenses of operating the store. Even though the margin of profit is usually small, it is nevertheless built into the price of every item purchased by the customer. The accidental overrings that slip by uncorrected are a result of human nature. We all make mistakes.

If we can't bring along someone to help us shop, and we can't watch the clerk ring up every item, and we can't keep the clerk from making mistakes, just what can we do to keep from overpaying at the checkstand? Not much. But we can use the electronic calculator to total our purchases before we arrive at the checkstand. Then we know if mistakes are happening. If we consistently are overcharged, there's no doubt we will find something to do about it, using our own ingenuity.

SALES TAX

Some states require retailers to charge a sales tax on nonfood items, but exempt food items entirely from the tax. At the checkout counter, the clerks add the tax as each taxable item passes through. Tax rate tables in most states are prepared to guarantee that if the retailer collects the amount shown on the table, he will collect no less than the sales tax required by law, but oftentimes more than the percentage tax required. For example, in California the sales tax is 5 percent. The tax on an item costing $0.20 is therefore $0.01. But the tax tables tell the retail clerks to charge $0.01 if an item is priced at $0.13. Eight $0.13 items rang up separately would cost $0.08 in tax plus $1.04 for the merchandise—a total of $1.12. The true sales tax on $1.04 should be $0.05—not $0.08—if the rate for sales tax in the state is 5 percent. To prevent an overcharge of sales tax at the checkout counter, place all taxable items on the counter first, and ask the checkout clerk to ring those items up first, subtotal the cost, and apply the sales tax to the subtotaled amount, rather than to each item individually. Over a period of a year, you may save enough to buy an extra carton of cigarettes. It's like getting something for nothing.

GROUPING AND PRICING

Grouping of items that are priced as three for $0.25, four for $0.15, etc. should be done when the items are placed on the checkout counter. If a clerk sees a single item priced at three for $0.25, he will ring it up at $0.09. When the two like items come through, each of those may be rang up at $0.09 each, because they were not grouped. In this case you have paid a total of $0.27 for the three items you thought you were going to pay $0.25 for, a whopping 8-percent increase in your food cost for those items. In addition to grouping your taxable items, it pays to group the group-priced items also.

One of the biggest fallacies of grocery shoppers is the belief that the giant economy size costs less per unit than the regular or small size. In one unit-pricing survey, almost half of the giant economy sizes checked cost as much as, or more than, the regular sizes! Some items were **considerably** more expensive in the giant economy sizes, per unit of measure. We have devoted an entire chapter in this book to unit pricing—be sure you understand the basics of unit pricing. (You can find the unit price by dividing the price of the package by the number of ounces in the package.) We suggest that you review the unit-pricing chapter right now. You'll save a lot if you unit-price your purchases.

The next time you embark on that great adventure at the supermarket, be armed with the electronic calculator. It may be no pleasure to notice how much prices have increased from your last visit to the market, but you at least will have the pleasure of knowing that you've shopped as wisely as possible.

PREPARATIONS BEFORE VISITING THE SUPER-MARKET

The best electronic calculator to use when visiting the supermarket is the small hand-held type. If a wrist type of calculator is ever developed, it would be even better, because it would free both hands for the cart and the groceries. In the meantime, we must use what is available. The ideal situation is to carefully fasten the calculator to the upper left corner of a standard letter-size clipboard. On the remaining space on the clipboard, attach a small pad of paper, making sure it is large enough to record various figures used in your calculations and your running total of groceries purchased. Be sure to have a pencil with you.

The clipboard can be placed in the shopping cart when not in use. The cart will protect the calculator from accidental abuse or dropping. Clipboards and tablets can be purchased in most supermarkets or stationery stores.

METHODS OF CALCULATING GROCERY PURCHASES

How many times have you wondered if you had enough cash to pay for all the groceries you've put in the shopping cart? You wanted to buy a little extra milk, to save yourself another trip tomorrow, but do you have enough to pay for it?

Using the electronic calculator, keeping a running total is a cinch. You can even figure how much you're going to have left (if any) after the cashier gets through with you.

Precalculating your grocery bill has two advantages. It brings to your attention the price of each item you are placing in your shopping cart, so that you can check the checker, and it enables you to compare the total you have calculated with the total you pay at the checkout counter. Both of these procedures can save you money, as we pointed out.

Pricing each item as it is placed in the shopping cart has an added advantage. How often have you been at the checkout counter and found to your amazement that you've just purchased a package of goodies that cost much more than you thought it should cost? Often, perhaps. Now, when you pick up an item, you will not place it in the cart until you know the price. If the price is outrageous, as the price of some items is, you can reject the item on the spot!

There are several methods of figuring the exact cost of your grocery purchases before you reach the checkout counter. Some are more convenient than others, but each will result in almost precisely the same total as the cash register total. Any variations are the result of approximations in sales taxes, or some other items we have previously pointed out in this chapter. The methods we are going to discuss in this chapter are: (1) the list method, where we list the taxable and nontaxable items, (2) the method whereby we calculate the price of each item, including tax, as it is placed in the shopping cart, (3) the method whereby the tax is calculated just before we check out, (4) the preplanned-shopping method, and (5) the lazy man's method. The rich man's method, which we are not going to discuss in detail, is the method whereby two electronic calculators are used. One is used to calculate tax, compute unit prices, and evaluate multiple purchases (such as seven items at $0.29 each), and to do other miscellaneous side calculations. The other calculator simply keeps a running total. Some of the more expensive models have two memories, and only one of these is required in the rich man's method. You can probably come up with other methods than those below, with a little experimentation.

List Method

As each item is placed in the shopping cart, the price of that item is written on a pad of paper. Two columns are used—one for the taxable items and one for the nontaxable items. After the last item is put in the shopping cart, each column is added up separately on the electronic calculator. The taxable

total is then multiplied by the tax factor, which is 1 plus the tax rate expressed in decimal form. (For example, if the sales tax is 5 percent, the decimal form of the tax rate is 0.05, and the tax factor is 1.05.) Add the product of this multiplication (the taxed total) to the nontax total. You will obtain a **grand total**, which is the amount you should have to pay at the checkout counter. A variation of this method is to simply multiply the taxable items by the sales tax rate (expressed as a decimal) to obtain the sales tax amount, and then add the taxable item total, the nontaxable total, and the sales tax to arrive at the grand total. The advantages of using the list method and its variations are that it is easy and accurate, and it frees the calculator to perform unit-pricing checks and other calculations.

Figuring Exact Cost of Groceries (List Method)

After loading her shopping cart, Mrs. Washington finds that she has made these two lists on her tablet:

Nontax items	Taxable items
$ 0.80	$ 1.77
5.00	1.38
0.87	0.25
0.48	0.77
0.22	0.54
0.35	0.25

The sales tax rate in her state is 5 percent. How much should she pay at the checkout counter?

Procedure

Operation	Keyboard Entry	Function Touch	Display	Description
Set decimal to three places				
Clear registers and display		C	0.000	
Enter first nontax item price	.8	+	0.800	
Enter second nontax item price	5	+	5.800	Running total
Enter third nontax item price	.87	+	6.670	Running total
Enter fourth nontax item price	.48	+	7.150	Running total
Enter fifth nontax item price	.22	+	7.370	Running total

134

Operation	Keyboard Entry	Function Touch	Display	Description
Enter sixth nontax item price	.35	+	7.720	Nontax item total (record)
Clear registers and display		C	0.000	
Enter first tax item	1.77	+	1.770	Running total
Enter second tax item	1.38	+	3.150	Running total
Enter third tax item	.25	+	3.400	Running total
Enter fourth tax item	.77	+	4.170	Running total
Enter fifth tax item	.54	+	4.710	Nontaxable total
Enter sixth tax item	.25	+	4.960	
Transfer display to multiply register	None	x	4.960	
Enter tax factor (1 plus decimal rate)	1.05	=	5.208	Taxable item total
Transfer display to add register	None	+	5.208	
Enter nontax item total	7.72	+	12.928	Answer

Mrs. Washington should pay $12.93 at the checkstand.

Figuring Tax and Total As You Shop

If you have a limited amount of funds with you, this method gives you the accumulated total every instant, at the time you place the item in the shopping cart. And it is simple to follow. It requires figuring the price of each item, including sales tax if any, as it is taken from the shelf, and adding that figure to the previously accumulated total. Since the calculator is also being used for unit-pricing calculations, a running total is not maintained in the calculator, but is written on a scratch pad.

Figuring Exact Cost of Groceries (Tax and Total)

Mrs. Adams puts the following items into her shopping cart, in order:

1. Twenty cans of orange juice at $0.48 each
2. Two steaks for $1.69 and $3.11
3. Four loaves of bread at $0.41 each
4. One broom for $3.39

The sales tax rate in Mrs. Adams' state is 4⅝ percent on nonfood items. How much will Mrs. Adams pay at the checkout counter?

Procedure

Operation	Keyboard Entry	Function Touch	Display	Description
Set decimal to five places				
Clear registers and display		C	0.00000	To take care of exotic sales tax rate
Enter numerator of tax rate fraction	5	÷	5.00000	
Enter denominator of tax rate fraction	8	=	0.62500	
Transfer display to add register	None	+	0.62500	
Enter whole-number part of tax rate	4	+	4.62500	Percentage sales tax rate
Transfer display to divide register	None	÷	4.62500	
Enter conversion factor (from percentage to decimal)	100	=	0.04625	Decimal sales tax rate
Transfer display to add register	None	+	0.04625	
Enter principal factor	1	+	1.04625	Tax factor (record)
Clear registers and display		C	0.00000	
Enter quantity	20	x	20.00000	Item 1 quantity
Enter price each	.48	=	9.60000	Item 1 total (dollars)
Transfer display to add register	None	+	9.60000	
Enter price	1.69	+	11.29000	Item 2, first steak, running total
Enter price	3.11	+	14.40000	Item 2, second steak, running total
Clear registers and display		C	0.00000	(record)
Enter quantity	4	x	4.00000	Item 3 quantity
Enter price each	.41	=	1.64000	Item 3 cost
Transfer display to add register	None	+	1.64000	
Enter running total	14.4	+	16.04000	Item 3 running total (record)
Clear registers and display		C	0.00000	
Enter price	3.39	x	3.39000	Item 4 price before tax
Enter tax factor	1.04625	=	3.54679	Item 4 cost with tax
Transfer display to add register	None	+	3.54679	
			19.58679	
Enter running total	16.04	+		Answer

Mrs. Adams will pay $19.59 at the checkstand.

Running-Total Method With Tax Calculation Before Checkout

With this method, the price of every item is entered in the electronic calculator as it is placed in the shopping cart, without regard to the sales tax. A list of the cost of taxable items is written on a pad of paper for later calculations. A running total of the items purchased is always on display on the electronic calculator. Just before you arrive at the checkout counter, you calculate the sales tax and add it to the running total. An example follows.

Grocery Cost Calculation (Running Total Method)

Mrs. Jefferson puts the following items in her shopping cart in the order given:

1. Two dozen eggs at $0.71 a dozen
2. Four bunches of carrots at $0.18 a bunch
3. One can of weed killer at $1.89
4. A 10 lb bag of potatoes at $0.89 a bag
5. One apron at $1.19

The sales tax rate in Mrs. Jefferson's state is 4 percent on nonfood items. How much will Mrs. Jefferson's purchases cost?

Procedure

Operation	Keyboard Entry	Function Touch	Display	Description
Set decimal to two places				
Clear registers and display		C	0.00	
Enter price	.71	+	0.71	Item 1, first dozen (dollars)
Enter price	.71	+	1.42	Item 1, second dozen. running total
Enter price	.18	+	1.60	Item 2, first bunch. running total
Enter price	.18	+	1.78	Item 2, second bunch. running total
Enter price	.18	+	1.96	Item 2, third bunch. running total
Enter price	.18	+	2.14	Item 2, fourth bunch. running total
Enter price	1.89	+	4.03	Item 3, running total (Item 3 is a taxable item and is written on the pad)
Enter price	.89	+	4.92	Item 4 running total
Enter price	1.19	+	6.11	Total of all items before tax (record on pad)
Clear registers and display		C	0.00	

Operation	Keyboard Entry	Function Touch	Display	Description
Enter price of item 3	1.89	+	1.89	Taxable item
Enter price of item 5	1.19	+	3.08	Total of taxable items
Transfer display to multiply register	None	x	3.08	
Enter sales tax rate expressed as a decimal	.04	=	0.12	Sales tax
Transfer to add register	None	+	0.12	
Enter total of all items before sales tax calculation	6.11	+	6.23	Total purchases including tax

Mrs. Jefferson will pay $6.23, including tax, at the checkout counter.

Preplanned-Shopping Method

The advantage of this method is that very little recording on a pad of paper is necessary, and a running total is kept. The running total is exact—it includes sales tax, after the purchase of the taxable items is completed. The method is to select all taxable items from the shelves before any nontaxable items are placed in the shopping cart. As soon as the taxable-item shopping is complete, the tax is calculated. From that point forward, an exact running total is maintained as each item is placed in the cart, and the display obtained when the last item is selected will be the total at the checkout counter.

Grocery Costing (Preplanned-Shopping Method)

Mrs. Madison puts the following items into her shopping cart in the order shown:

1. An egg-beater for $2.59
2. Three pairs of shoes at $2 a pair
3. Three dog leashes at $1.62 each
4. Seven wastebaskets at $2.88 each
5. A garden hose at $5.50
6. A chair for $10.98
7. Four steaks totaling $11.78
8. 2.6 lb of apples at $0.44 a pound
9. Three bunches of carrots at $0.19 a bunch
10. Two lollipops at $0.04 each
11. A six-pack of grape juice for $0.84
12. Eight cans of soup at $0.34 each

The sales tax rate in Mrs. Madison's state is 5 percent on nonfood items. How much will Mr. Madison pay when she checks out?

SUMMIT MODEL SQR16M—This instrument is a major step forward in miniature electronic calculators. The **square root** feature and **memory** system make this little powerhouse especially useful for technical mathematics. True algebraic logis permits direct negative entries. Square roots are calculated with a single key, while another single key performs memory storage and retrieval. The decimal key presets the decimal in positions 0 to 7. Additionally, the SQR16M features automatic roundoff and full floating decimal systems.

The unit weighs 8¼ ounces, while its shirt-pocket size makes it ideal for holding and operating in one hand. It has 8-digit entry and display, with 16-digit calculating capacity, zero suppression, automatic overflow protection, true credit balance; it performs mixed and chain calculations allowing addition, subtraction, multiplication, or division to the original figure without reentry. The calculator is fully functional on ac or dc. Built-in ni-cad batteries provide 10 hours of continuous use, and batteries recharge in only 3 hours. The unit has a battery-saving device in which the display turns off automatically after 15 seconds, but the last figure can easily be recalled. It comes with an ac charger and a deluxe carrying pouch. It is guaranteed for one year. **Summit International Corporation,** 180 West 2950 South, Salt Lake City, Utah 84115.

Procedure

Operation	Keyboard Entry	Function Touch	Display	Description
Set decimal to two places				
Clear registers and display		C	0.00	
Enter price	2.59	+	2.59	Item 1
Enter price	6	+	8.59	Item 2 running total
Enter price	1.62	+	10.21	Item 3, first leash
Enter price	1.62	+	11.83	Item 3, second leash
Enter price	1.62	+	13.45	Item 3, third leash
Enter price	2.88	+	16.33	Item 4, first basket
Enter price	2.88	+	19.21	Item 4, second basket
Enter price	2.88	+	22.09	Item 4, third basket
Enter price	2.88	+	24.97	Item 4, fourth basket
Enter price	2.88	+	27.85	Item 4, fifth basket
Enter price	2.88	+	30.73	Item 4, sixth basket
Enter price	2.88	+	33.61	Item 4, seventh basket
Enter price	5.5	+	39.11	Item 5
Enter price	10.98	+	50.09	Item 6 taxable total
Transfer display to multiply register	None	x	50.09	
Enter tax factor (1 plus decimal rate)	1.05	=	52.59	Taxable total with tax
Transfer display to add register	None	+	52.59	Taxable total with tax
Enter price	11.78	+	64.37	Item 7 running total (record)
Clear registers and display		C	0.00	
Enter quantity	2.6	x	2.60	Item 8 quantity
Enter price	.44	=	1.14	Item 8 cost
Transfer display to add register	None	+	1.14	
Enter running total	64.37	+	65.51	Item 8 running total
Enter price	.19	+	65.70	Item 9, first bunch
Enter price	.19	+	65.89	Item 9, second bunch
Enter price	.19	+	66.08	Item 9, third bunch
Enter price	.08	+	66.16	Item 10
Enter price	.84	+	67.00	Item 11

Operation	Keyboard Entry	Function Touch	Display	Description
Enter price	1.70	+	68.70	Item 12, first five cans
Enter price	.34	+	69.04	Item 12, sixth can
Enter price	.34	+	69.38	Item 12, seventh can
Enter price	.34	+	69.72	Answer

Mrs. Madison should pay $69.72 at the check stand. If she had taken a whole number of pounds of apples in item 8, she would not have had to interrupt her additive calculation, and she would not have had to use pencil and paper at all. However, if she had desired to unit-price any of the items when purchased, it would have been necessary to record the display total, and pick up that amount when she entered the next item.

Lazy Man's Method

When this method is used, each and every item is entered in the electronic calculator and a running total is kept, regardless of whether the item is taxable or not. If no taxable items have been purchased, then the display on the calculator will be the price that must be paid at the checkout counter. If any taxable items at all have been placed in the cart, calculate sales tax on the entire running total. When you check out, you will feel pleased that the checkout clerk charged you less than you had on your electronic calculator.

Grocery Calculation

Mr. Monroe throws the following items into his shopping cart in this order:

1. Two packs of razor blades at $1.29 each
2. Six watermelons at $0.99 each
3. Six cantaloupes at three for a dollar
4. Twenty-six cans of pineapple juice at $0.28 each
5. Three pounds American cheese for a total of $2.79
6. A flashlight for $2.25
7. Eight batteries at $0.48 each
8. Two cans of soup at $0.11 each
9. A ham for $3.14
10. Eight steaks totaling $24.11
11. 18 lb 1 oz of oranges at 7 lb for a dollar
12. 14 cans of tuna at $0.66 each

The sales tax rate in Mr. Monroe's state is a whopping 6½ percent on nonfood items. Mr. Monroe makes the following calculations on his electronic calculator as he shops.

SUMMIT MODEL MR8—This little electronic calculator lets you whiz through a multistep problem by keeping a running total in its add-on, discount memory. This system makes your work simple as you figure manufacturing costs, special purchase discounts, taxes and commissions, profit margins, retail markups, sales tax calculations, unit pricing while grocery shopping, and a host of other multifunction calculations that require subtotals and a grand total. To accumulate subtotals, press the M=function key conveniently located on top of the calculator, instead of the=key. The subtotal that appears on the display can then be added or subtracted into the memory by pressing the + or − key. The display will now show your running total.

Direct negative entry and a negative sign in the display permit operations involving mixed signs, yielding true credit balance answers. A percent key lets you quickly solve problems involving percentages. Its fully floating decimal system can be preset in any position from 0 to 7 to automatically round off your answer. Automatic constant makes repeat multiplication and division easy. The unit features an 8-digit display, but it will calculate internally with up to 16 digits. If the result is more than 8 digits, the keyboard locks to prevent errors and an overflow symbol appears in the display until the keyboard is cleared.

Built-in ni-cad batteries recharge in just 3 hours to give 10 hours of operating time. To conserve battery energy, the readout automatically shuts off after holding the same number for 15 seconds and a tiny symbol appears to indicate that the calculator is still on. The last number is recalled by simply pressing the **equal** key. The unit weighs only 8¼ ounces and measures 2¾ x 4 x 1⅛ inches. Each calculator is delivered with an ac charger and a deluxe padded carrying pouch. **Summit International Corporation, 180 West 2950 South, Salt Lake City, Utah 84115.**

Procedure

Operation	Keyboard Entry	Function Touch	Display	Description
Set decimal to three places				To take care of exotic sales tax rate
Clear registers and display		C	0.000	
Enter price	2.58	+	2.580	Item 1 (dollars)
Enter price	5.94	+	8.520	Item 2 running total
Enter price	2	+	10.520	Item 3 running total (record)
Clear registers and display		C	0.000	
Enter quantity	26	x	26.000	Item 4 quantity
Enter price	.28	=	7.280	Item 4 cost
Transfer display to add register	None	+	7.280	
Enter running total	10.52	+	17.800	Item 4 running total
Enter price	2.79	+	20.590	Item 5
Enter price	2.25	+	22.840	Item 6 running total (record)
Clear registers and display		C	0.000	
Enter quantity	8	x	8.000	Item 7 quantity
Enter price	.48	=	3.840	Item 7 cost
Transfer display to add register	None	+	3.840	
Enter running total	22.84	+	26.680	Item 7 running total
Enter price	.22	+	26.900	Item 8
Enter price	3.14	+	30.040	Item 9
Enter price	24.11	+	54.150	Item 10 running total (record)
Clear registers and display		C	0.000	
Enter price	1	÷	1.000	Item 11 price for 7 lb
Enter divisor	7	=	0.143	Item 11 unit price
Transfer display to multiply register	None	x	0.143	
Enter quantity	18.062	=	2.580	Item 11 cost
Transfer display to add register	None	+	2.580	
Enter running total	54.15	+	56.730	Item 11 running total (record)
Clear registers and display		C	0.000	
Enter quantity	14	x	14.000	Item 12 quantity
Enter price	.66	=	9.240	Item 12 cost

143

Operation	Keyboard Entry	Function Touch	Display	Description
Transfer display to add register	None	+	9.240	
Enter running total	56.73	+	65.97	Total without tax
Transfer display to multiply register	None	x	65.97	
Enter tax factor (1 plus decimal rate)	1.065	=	70.258	Overestimated total

Prepared to pay as much as $70.26, Mr. Monroe is pleased to find that the checkout clerk charges him only $66.53

Kitchen Uses of the Electronic Calculator

My wife had a recipe for tipsy pudding (my favorite) that would serve four people, and since we were having guests for dinner, she needed to know the quantity of ingredients required to make seven servings. I determined the correct quantity of each ingredient with the electronic calculator, and then began to ask a few questions about cooking. I found that there are hundreds of calculator applications in the kitchen. My wife told me that the problem of calculating the correct amount of ingredients arises frequently. Usually, she told me, she just doubles the amount called for in the recipe if she has guests. She always has more than enough, and often she throws the leftovers away in a day or two. What a waste, I thought.

The next day, my wife told me of some foreign recipes she had but was unable to use. She was unable to use any of them because of the units of **measurement** were in strange words— even though the recipe was written in English. Upon examining the recipes, I found that the "strange" words were merely metric units of measure—not really strange at all. The idea began to creep into my head that perhaps I should include a chapter on kitchen uses of the electronic calculator, especially when I checked with my neighbors and found that they had the same problems.

One of my neighbors told me that she had a British cook-book, but when she followed the recipes to the letter, the resulting dishes never seemed to turn out right. After a little research, I found that the British measurements are not the same as the American measurements! A British cup contains 20 British tablespoons, whereas the American cup contains only 16 American tablespoons. In addition, the British and American cups are not the same size. And neither are the tablespoons. It's no wonder the British recipes didn't turn out right. It's just that our American neighbor didn't know what the British meant when the British recipe called for four and one-half cups of flour. That's really five and one-half cups of American flour (five cups six and one-half teaspoons, to be exact).

Clearly, the calculator is as important a cooking tool in the kitchen as the electric mixer is—no modern kitchen should be without either.

INCREASING SERVINGS FROM RECIPES

One of the major problems of the kitchen is in increasing the amount of ingredients in a recipe when the number of servings is to be increased. It is usually fairly easy to double the ingredients if the number of servings is to be approximately doubled, although this approach may not be economical if it makes more servings than there are eaters. A ratio can be established between the number of servings provided in the recipe, and the number of servings desired. The result is the desired relationship between the number of servings desired and the amount of food prepared.

We must keep in mind, however, that cooking is not an exact science. In cooking, the exact measurement down to the ounce is not necessary when we are dealing with cups, pints, etc. A certain amount of rounding is permissible. In fact, it is often mandatory, because cooks have no time to measure each and every ingredient to the nearest drop.

Let's look at a problem where Mrs. Polk desires to serve 17 people 4 servings each, but the recipe is designed to provide only 24 servings.

Expanding a Recipe

Mr. and Mrs. Polk, who live alone, are having 15 guests for dinner. Each person is to receive four servings of eggnog. Mrs. Polk has a recipe for 24 servings of eggnog requiring the following ingredients: 8 eggs, 1 cup of sugar, ½ tsp (teaspoon) of salt, 3 pints of milk, 2 tsp of vanilla, and 6 tbsp (tablespoons) of sugar.

Allowing 10 percent extra for spillage and eggnog gluttons, how much of each ingredient should Mrs. Polk use?

Procedure

Operation	Keyboard Entry	Touch Function	Display	Description
Set decimal to three places				
Clear registers and display		C	0.000	
Enter number of persons at dinner	17	x	17.000	
Enter number of servings for each person	4	=	68.000	Total number of servings desired
Transfer display to multiply register	None	x	68.000	

Operation	Keyboard Entry	Function Touch	Display	Description
Enter spillage factor (1 plus decimal rate)	1.10	=	74.800	
Transfer display to add register	None	+	74.800	
Enter 0.2 (to make whole number)	.2	+	75.000	Total number of servings required (rounded up)
Transfer display to divide register	None	÷	75.000	Ratio of servings required to servings in recipe (record)
Enter servings in recipe	24	=	3.125	Constant multiplier
Transfer display to multiply register	None	x	3.125	Eggs required (record)
Enter number of eggs from recipe	8	=	25.000	
Clear registers and display		C	0.000	
Enter number of pints of milk from recipe	3	x	3.000	
Enter constant multiplier	3.125	=	9.375	Milk required, in pints (record whole number 9 as 1 gal 1 pt)
Clear registers and display		C	0.000	
Enter fraction from required milk pints	.375	x	0.375	
Enter conversion factor (cups in a pint)	2	=	0.750	Rest of milk required (record entire milk requirement as 1 gal 1 pt 3/4 cup)
Clear registers and display		C	0.000	
Enter number of cups of sugar from recipe	1	x	1.000	
Enter constant multiplier	3.125	=	3.125	Sugar required in cups (record)
Clear registers and display		C	0.000	
Enter sugar fraction	.125	x	0.125	
Enter conversion factor (tablespoons in a cup)	16	=	2.000	Sugar fraction in tablespoons (record entire sugar requirement as 3 cups 2 tbsp)
Clear registers and display		C	0.000	
Enter number of spoons of vanilla from recipe	2	x	2.000	
Enter constant multiplier	3.125	=	6.250	Vanilla required (record as 6 1/4 tsp)
Clear registers and display		C	0.000	
Enter amount of salt from recipe	0.5	x	0.500	
Enter constant multiplier	3.125	=	1.562	Salt required (record as 1 1/2 tsp)
Clear registers and display		C	0.000	

Operation	Keyboard Entry	Function Touch	Display	Description
Enter second call for sugar from recipe	6	x	6.000	
Enter constant multiplier	3.125	=	18.750	Second sugar requirement (record as 1 cup plus 2 3/4 tbsp)

Mrs. Polk transfers these numbers to her cookbook, and her recipe for 75 servings of eggnog now reads: 25 eggs, 3 cups 2 tbsp of sugar, 1½ tsp of salt, 1 gal 1 pt ¾ cup of milk, 6¼ tsp of vanilla, and 1 cup 2¾ tbsp of sugar.

DECREASING SERVINGS FROM RECIPES

The previous problem dealt with increasing the servings from the number given in the recipe. If we want to decrease the number of servings, we must again set up a ratio between the number of servings provided in the recipe, and the number of servings desired. As we stated before, exact measurements are not usually required in cooking, when we are using measurements in cups, pints, etc,; but when the amounts of the ingredients are being reduced, as in the example that follows, we are required to be a bit more cautious in our calculating and measuring.

In the following problem, Mrs. Taylor must not only reduce the amount of ingredients, she must also determine the size of the pan.

Reducing a Recipe

Mrs. Taylor wishes to make 20 fudge bars. Her recipe calls for a 20 in. by 10 in. by 2 in. pan and the following ingredients for 100 fudge bars: 9 tbsp of butter, 12½ cups of Rice Crispies, 1½ tsp of salt, 13 oz of semisweet chocolate, 1 lb 9 oz of marshmallows, ¾ cup of walnut meats, and 1½ cups of chopped coconut meat.

What size pan and how much of each ingredient should she use?

Procedure

Operation	Keyboard Entry	Function Touch	Display	Description
Set decimal to four places				
Clear registers and display		C	0.0000	
Enter quantity desired	20	÷	20.0000	
Enter quantity in recipe	100	=	0.2000	Ratio of bars required to bars in recipe (record)
Transfer display to multiply register	None	x	0.2000	Constant multiplier

Operation	Keyboard Entry	Function Touch	Display	Description
Enter pan area in square inches	200	=	40.0000	Pan area required, in square inches (record)
Clear registers and display		C	0.0000	
Enter butter multiplicand	9	x	9.0000	
Enter constant multiplier	.2	=	1.8000	Butter required, in tablespoons.
Transfer display to multiply register	None	x	1.8000	
Enter conversion factor (tablespoons to teaspoons)	3	=	5.4000	Butter required, in teaspoons (record as 5 $1/2$ tsp or as 1 tbsp 2 $1/2$ tsp)
Clear registers and display		C	0.0000	
Enter marshmallow multiplicand (ounces)	25	x	25.0000	
Enter constant multiplier	.2		5.0000	Marshmallow requirement, in ounces (record)
Clear registers and display		C	0.0000	
Enter Rice Crispies multiplicand	12.5	x	12.5000	
Enter constant multiplier	.2	=	2.5000	Rice Crispies required in cups (record as 2 $1/2$ cups)
Clear registers and display		C	0.0000	
Enter walnut multiplicand (cups)	.75	x	0.7500	
Enter constant multiplier	.2	=	0.1500	Walnuts required, in cups
Transfer display to multiply register	None	x	0.1500	
Enter conversion factor (teaspoons in a cup)	48	=	7.2000	Walnuts required, in teaspoons (record as 2 tbsp 1 $1/4$ tsp)
Clear registers and display		C	0.0000	
Enter salt multiplicand	1.5	x	1.5000	
Enter constant multiplier	.2	=	0.3000	Salt required, in teaspoons (record salt as $1/4$ tsp; coconut as $1/4$ cup)
Clear registers and display		C	0.000	
Enter chocolate multiplicand	13	x	13.0000	
Enter constant multiplier	.2	=	2.6000	Chocolate required, in ounces (record as 2 $1/2$ oz)

Mrs. Taylor now adds the recipe for 20 fudge bars to her cookbook: 8 in. by 5 in. by 2 in. pan, 1 tbsp 2½ tsp of butter, 2½ cups of Rice Crispies, ¼ tsp of salt, 2½ oz of semisweet chocolate, 5 oz of marshmallows, 2 tbsp 1¼ tsp of walnut meats, and ¼ cup of chopped coconut meat.

TRANSLATING BRITISH RECIPES TO AMERICAN MEASURES

A British girl trying to cook from an American recipe is going to have as much trouble as an American trying to cook from a British recipe. No matter how careful she is and how hard she tries, something seems to go wrong every time. The trouble is not in the way the cooking is done, nor in the method of preparation or mixing. It's just that British measurements are not the same as American measurements. Here's how Mrs. Lincoln solved the problem.

British to U.S. Units Conversion*

Mrs. Lincoln received a British cookbook as a Christmas gift. She was troubled by the fact that the British cup contains 20 British tablespoons, while the U.S. cup contains 16 U.S. tablespoons. The British and U.S. cups are not the same size, and neither are the British and U.S. tablespoons. She decided to convert some of her recipes to U.S. measure using her electronic calculator. The first recipe she converted—for Cornwall cake—had the following ingredients: 4½ cups of flour, 1 tsp of salt, 3 tsp of flavoring, 3 cups of sugar, 1 cup of shortening, 1 cup of egg (3 eggs), 6 tsp of baking soda, and 2 cups of milk.

Procedure

Operation	Keyboard Entry	Function Touch	Display	Description
Set decimal to four places				
Clear registers and display		C		
Enter flour (British cups)	4.5	x	0.0000	
Enter conversion factor (British to U.S. cups)	1.2009	=	4.5000	Flour (U.S. cups)
Transfer display to multiply register	None	x	5.4040	
Enter conversion factor (U.S. cups to U.S. tablespoons)	16	=	5.4040	Flour (U.S. tablespoons—record as U.S. 5 cups 6 ½ tbsp)
Clear registers and display		C	86.4648	
Enter sugar (British cups)	3	x	0.0000	
Enter conversion factor	1.2009	=	3.0000	.Sugar (U.S. cups)
Transfer display to multiply register	None	x	3.6027	
*Enter conversion factor (U.S. cups to U.S. tablespoons)	16	=	3.6027	Sugar (U.S. tablespoons—record as U.S. 3 cups 9 ½ tbsp)

*To avoid confusion, hereinafter, we'll refer to the **English** system as the U.S. system.

Operation	Keyboard Entry	Function Touch	Display	Description
Clear registers and display		C	57.6432	
Enter soda (British teaspoons)	6	x	0.0000	
Enter conversion factor (British to U.S. teaspoons)	.7206	=	6.0000	Soda (U.S. teaspoons—record as 4 $1/3$ U.S. tsp of baking soda)
Clear registers and display		C	4.3236	
Enter salt (British teaspoon)	1	x	0.0000	
Enter conversion factor (British to U.S. teaspoons)	.7206	=	1.0000	Salt (U.S. teaspoons—record as $3/4$ U.S. tsp)
Clear registers and display		C	0.7206	
Enter shortening (1 British cup)	1	x	0.0000	
Enter conversion factor (British to U.S. cups)	1.2009	=	1.0000	Shortening (U.S. cups)
Transfer display to multiply register	None	x	1.2009	
Enter conversion factor (U.S. cups to U.S. tablespoons)	16	=	1.2009	Shortening or egg (U.S. tablespoons—record as U.S. 1 cup 3 $1/4$ tbsp)
Clear registers and display		C	19.2144	
Enter milk (British cups)	2	x	0.0000	
Enter conversion factor	1.2009	=	2.0000	Milk (U.S. cups)
Transfer display to multiply register	None	x	2.4018	
Enter conversion factor	16	=	2.4018	Milk (U.S. tablespoons—record as U.S. 2 cups 6 $1/2$ tbsp)
Clear registers and display			38.4288	
Enter flavoring (British teaspoons)	3	x	3.0000	
Enter conversion factor (British to U.S. teaspoons)	.7206	=	2.1618	Flavoring (U.S. teaspoons—record as 2 $1/4$ U.S. tsp)

Mrs. Lincoln now rewrites the ingredients for her English recipe as follows: 5 cups 6½ tbsp of flour, 3 cups 9½ tbsp of sugar, 4½ tsp of baking soda, ¾ tsp of salt, 1 cup 3¼ tbsp of shortening, 2 cups 6½ tbsp of milk, 2¼ tsp of flavoring, and 3 eggs.

CONVERTING METRIC RECIPES TO U.S. MEASURES

Thousands of fantastic recipes are found in foreign cookbooks, but the average American housewife has no idea of how to use them. If the recipe is in a foreign language, the hardest job by far is in translating the recipe to English. Using the electronic calculator to convert metric units to standard U.S. cooking measurements is much easier done than said.

151

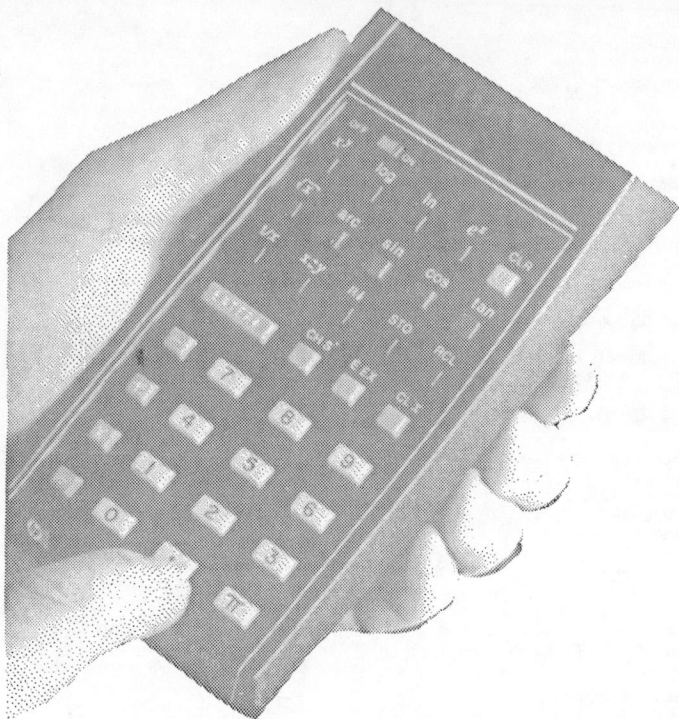

HEWLETT PACKARD MODEL HP-35—Hewlett Packard's HP-35 is a scientific-language pocket calculator that combines slide rule portability with the precise accuracy and problem-solving power of a small computer. You can compute transcendental functions with exceptional accuracy in less than half a second, yet the unit is as easy to operate as an adding machine.

The HP-35 is a 35-key, pocket-size scientific and engineering calculator that performs logarithmic, trigonometric, and mathematical functions with single keystrokes and eliminates the need to refer to log or trig tables. It displays up to 10 significant decimal digits and automatically positions the decimal point throughout its 200-decade calculation range (10^{-99} to 10^{99}). It combines the portability and convenience of the slide rule with the problem-solving power of a desktop scientific calculator. Of course, it provides answers in a fraction of the time required for slide rule calculation.

A series of specific functions or formulas are preprogramed into the HP-35 to provide its unique capability for performing trignometric and exponential functions with single keystrokes. This feature makes it unnecessary to refer to tables for the values of these functions: add, subtract, multiply, divide, square root, sin x, cos x, tan x, arc sin x, arc cos x, arc tan x, $\log_{10}$ x, $\log_e$ x, e^x, xy, $1/x$, pi, and data storage and positioning keys.

The unit, which is ac or dc operated, is provided with an "operational stack" of 4 registers, plus a memory register for constants. The stack is used for solving either simple or complex problems that require intermediate values. The entire unit measures about 5¾ x 3¼ x 1 inch and weighs 9 ounces. **Hewlett Packard, 10900 Wolfe Road, Cupertino, Calif. 95014.**

Metric to U.S. Units Conversion

Miss Fillmore has translated the following recipe for "tuna goodies" from a Norwegian cookbook: One 250-gram can of tuna, 60 ml (milliliters) of chopped celery, 60 ml of mayonnaise, 60 ml of horseradish, 160 ml of butter, 2 ml of pepper, 7 ml of chopped onion, and 20 toast strips.

Now she is going to use the electronic calculator to do her arithmetic to get the amounts into units that fit her kitchen utensils. To do this she uses the following numerical relations:

$$1 \text{ gram} = 0.03527 \text{ oz} \quad 1 \text{ ml} = 0.2029 \text{ tsp} = 0.004227 \text{ cup}$$

Procedure

Operation	Keyboard Entry	Function Touch	Display	Description
Set decimal to five places				
Clear registers and display		C	0.00000	
Enter grams of tuna	250	x	250.00000	
Enter conversion factor	0.03527	=	8.81750	Ounces of tuna (record answer as 9)
Clear registers and display		C	0.00000	
Enter milliliters of celery	60	x	60.00000	Cups of celery
Enter conversion factor	.004227	=	0.25362	(record as 1/4 cup, and also record mayonnaise and horse-
Enter milliliters of butter	160	x	160.00000	radish as 1/4 cup each)
Enter conversion factor	.004227	=	0.67632	Cups of butter (record as 2/3 cup)
Clear registers and display		C	0.00000	
Enter milliliters of pepper	2	x	2.00000	
Enter conversion factor	.2029	=	0.40580	Teaspoons of pepper (record as 1/2 tsp)
Clear registers and display		C	0.00000	
Enter milliliters of onion	7	x	7.00000	
Enter conversion factor	.2029	=	1.42030	Teaspoons of onion (record as 1-1/2 tsp)

Miss Fillmore now rewrites her recipe for 40 "goodies" as follows: 9 oz of tuna, ¼ cup of chopped celery, ¼ cups of mayonnaise, ¼ cup of horseradish, ⅔ cup of butter, ½ teaspoon of pepper, 1½ tsp of chopped onion, and 20 toast strips.

Using a French Recipe

Mrs. Johnson has received the following recipe for fruitcake from her daughter in Paris: ½ kg (kilogram) dates, 1 kg cherries, 1 kg pecans, 1 kg pineapple, 500 ml

153

raisins, 1 kg mixed fruit, 400 ml butter, 1 liter sugar, 10 eggs, 1.6 liters cake flour, 8 ml baking soda, 5 ml salt, 11 ml vanilla, 11 ml nutmeg, 9 bananas, 250 ml buttermilk.

Procedure

Operation	Keyboard Entry	Function Touch	Display	Description
Set decimal to four places				
Clear registers and display		C	0.0000	
Enter kilograms of dates	.5	x	0.5000	
Enter conversion factor (kilograms to pounds)	2.2046	=	1.1023	Pounds of dates
Transfer display to multiply register	None	x	1.1023	
Enter conversion factor (pounds to ounces)		=	17.6368	Ounces of dates (record as 1 lb 1$\frac{3}{4}$ oz)
Clear registers and display		C	0.0000	
Enter kilograms of cherries		x	1.0000	
Enter conversion factor (kilograms to pounds)	2.2046	=	2.2046	Pounds of cherries
Transfer display to multiply register	None	x	2.2046	
Enter conversion factor (pounds to ounces)	16	=	35.2736	Ounces of cherries (record as 2 lb 3$\frac{1}{4}$ oz)
Clear registers and display		C	0.0000	
Enter milliliters of rasins	500	x	500.0000	
Enter conversion factor (milliliters to U.S. cups)	.0042	=	2.1000	Raisins U.S. cups
Transfer display to multiply register	None	x	2.1000	
Enter conversion factor (U.S. cups to U.S. tablespoons)	16	=	33.6000	Raisins (U.S. tablespoons– record as 2 cups 1$\frac{1}{2}$ tbsp)
Clear registers and display		C	0.0000	
Enter milliliters of butter	400	x	400.0000	
Enter conversion factor (milliliters to U.S. cups)	.0042	=	1.6800	Butter (U.S. cups)
Transfer display to multiply register	None	x	1.6800	
Enter conversion factor (U.S. cups to U.S. tablespoons)	16	=	26.8800	Butter U.S. tablespoons (record as 1 cup 11 tbsp)
Clear registers and display		C	0.0000	
Enter sugar	1	x	1.0000	

154

Operation	Keyboard Entry	Function Touch	Display	Description
Enter conversion factor (liters to U.S. cups)	4.2265	=	4.2265	Sugar (U.S. cups)
Transfer display to multiply register	None	x	4.2265	
Enter conversion factor (U.S. cups to U.S. tablespoons)	16	=	67.6240	Sugar (U.S. tablespoons—record as 4 cups $3\frac{1}{2}$ tbsp)
Clear registers and display		C	0.0000	
Enter liters of flour	1.6	x	1.6000	
Enter conversion factor (liters to U.S. cups)	4.2265	=	6.7624	Flour (U.S. cups—record as $6\frac{3}{4}$ cups)
Clear registers and display		C	0.0000	
Enter milliliters of soda	8	x	8.0000	
Enter conversion factor (milliliters to U.S. teaspoons)	.2029	=	1.6232	Soda (U.S. teaspoons—record as $1\frac{1}{2}$ U.S. tsp)
Clear registers and display		C	0.0000	
Enter milliliters of salt	5	x	5.0000	
Enter conversion factor	.2029	=	1.0145	Salt (U.S. teaspoons—record as 1 tsp)
Clear registers and display		C	0.0000	
Enter milliliters of vanilla	11	x	11.0000	
Enter conversion factor	.2029	=	2.2319	Vanilla (U.S. teaspoons—record as $2\frac{1}{4}$ tsp and record nutmeg in same amount)
Clear registers and display		C	0.0000	
Enter buttermilk milliliters	250	x	250.0000	
Enter conversion factor (milliliters to U.S. cups)	.0042	=	1.0500	Buttermilk (U.S. cups)
Transfer display to multiply register	None	x	1.0500	
Enter conversion factor (U.S. cups to U.S. tablespoons)	16	=	16.8000	Buttermilk (U.S. tablespoons—record as 1 cup $\frac{3}{4}$ tbsp)

Having completed the above calculations on her electronic calculator, Mrs. Johnson rewrites her fruitcake recipe using U.S. measures: 1 lb 1¾ oz dates, 2 lb 3¼ oz cherries, 2 lb 3¼ oz pecans, 2 lb 3¼ oz pineapple, 2 cups 1½ tbsp raisins, 2 lb 3¼ oz mixed fruit, 1 cup 11 tbsp butter, 4 cups 3½ tbsp sugar, 9 eggs, 6¾ cups cake flour, 1½ tsp baking soda, 1 tsp salt, 2¼ tsp vanilla, 2¼ tsp nutmeg, 9 bananas, 1 cup ¾ tbsp buttermilk.

CONVERTING COOKING TEMPERATURE FROM CELSIUS TO FAHRENHEIT

In many foreign cookbooks, the cooking temperatures are given in degrees Celsius. If we tried to use the temperature called for in the recipe on our Fahrenheit-graduated oven temperature scale, the food would never cook. One hundred degrees Celsius will boil water, but 100°F is no more than the temperature of a warm day. Using the electronic calculator, converting Celsius temperatures to Fahrenheit is quick and easy.

Converting Celsius Degrees to Fahrenheit Degrees

Mrs. Arthur's Transylvanian recipe for quiche lorraine calls for baking at 200°C. Her American oven is calibrated in degrees Fahrenheit. At what Fahrenheit temperature should she set her oven?

The equation for converting Celsius degree temperatures to Fahrenheit degree temperatures is

$$F = 1.8C + 32$$

Procedure

Operation	Keyboard Entry	Function Touch	Display	Description
Set decimal to four places				
Clear registers and display		C	0.0000	
Enter Celsius temperature	200	x	200.0000	
Enter conversion factor (Celsius to Fahrenheit)	1.8		360.0000	Fahrenheit degrees above freezing point of water
Transfer display to add register	None	+	360.0000	
Enter Fahrenheit scale adjustment (degrees)	32	+	392.0000	(Answer)

Mrs. Arthur should set her oven at 392°F.

CALORIE COUNTING

Many persons are calorie counters. If we know how many calories are in what we eat, it's easy to add up those calories on the electronic calculator.

Counting Calories with the Calculator

Mrs. Cleveland finds that she eats the following daily menu quite often:

Breakfast	Orange juice	8 oz	105 cal	
	Oatmeal	2 cups	300 cal	
	Milk	2 glasses	330 cal	
	Sugar	1 tsbp	45 cal	
	Egg	1	80 cal	
Lunch	Salad		140 cal	
	Lamb chop	½ lb	250 cal	
	Bread	2 slices	130 cal	
	Butter	2 squares	160 cal	
	Milk	1 glass	165 cal	
Supper	Roast beef	1 lb	240 cal	
	Baked potato	1 lb	140 cal	
	Butter	2 squares	160 cal	
	Green beans	1 cup	75 cal	
	Milk	2 glasses	330 cal	

What is her total calorie intake from each of the above meals and for the whole day?

Procedure

Operation	Keyboard Entry	Function Touch	Display	Description
Set decimal to zero places				
Clear registers and display		C	0	
Enter orange juice calories	105	+	105	
Enter oatmeal calories	300	+	405	Running total
Enter milk calories	330	+	735	Running total
Enter sugar calories	45	+	780	Running total
Enter egg calories	80	+	860	Breakfast total
				(record)
Clear registers and display		C	0	
Enter salad calories	140	+	140	Running total
Enter lamb calories	250	+	390	Running total
Enter bread calories	130	+	520	Running total
Enter butter calories	160	+	680	Lunch total
Enter milk calories	165	+	845	(record)
Clear registers and display		C	0	Running total
				Running total
Enter beef calories	240	+	240	Running total
Enter potato calories	140	+	380	Supper total
Enter butter calories	160	+	540	(record)
Enter bean calories	75	+	615	
Enter milk calories	330	+	945	Running total
Enter breakfast calories	860	+	1805	Daily total
Enter lunch calories	845	+	2650	(record)

Mrs. Cleveland's total calories for the day are:

Breakfast 860 cal
Lunch 845 cal
Supper 945 cal

One day 2650 cal

CALCULATING TRUE COST OF MEAT

Meat departments in the grocery store seem to be adding more and more fat to the cuts of meat they sell us. The housewife trims off the excess fat and throws it away (or feeds it to Rover), but that makes the cost of the edible meat that much more than the advertised price. A bargain in meat isn't a bargain if we have to discard a portion of it. It may be more economical to pay more per pound if the meat were trimmed by the butcher first.

Nowadays, even the bones seem bigger than usual (probably my imagination), but here is a problem Mrs. Davis had. She found a big bone, and just cut it out before cooking the meat. Let's see what she found.

High Cost of Dog Bones

Mrs. Davis bought a 4¼ lb chunk of meat at the store for $8.03. Back at the house she cut out the bone and put it on the kitchen scales. The bone weighed 1⅞ pounds. How much per pound did she pay for the meat itself?

Procedure

Operation	Keyboard Entry	Function Touch	Display	Description
Set decimal to four places				
Clear registers and display		C	0.0000	
Enter gross weight (pounds)	4.25	+	4.2500	
Enter bone weight (pounds)	1.875	−	2.3750	Net meat weight, in pounds (record)
Clear registers and display		C	0.0000	
Enter cost (dollars)	8.03	÷	8.0300	
Enter net meat weight (pounds)	2.375	=	3.3810	Net base price for meat (dollars per pound)

Mrs. David paid $3.38 per pound of meat.

KITCHEN CONVERSION TECHNIQUES

The super cooks seem to have a feel for conversions. My neighbor, Mrs. Woods, is a super cook—just about the best I've ever met. Her dinners are always a gourmet's delight. I asked

COLUMBIA "SCIENTIFIC" MODEL—The **Scientific** is an electronic pocket calculator that is two calculators in one, according to the manufacturer. It is a calculator for scientific and engineering use, and a business machine for all other normal calculations. The unit has an 8-digit LED display, a floating decimal system, a battery-saving device, and low-battery indicator. The batteries are rechargeable, but the unit can be operated on ac with the adapter. An underflow-overflow indicator prevents possible errors.

In addition to the four basic mathematical operations, the calculator will perform square root, automatic square, and reciprocal operations for scientific applications. For business or home use, the instrument has a built-in memory, percentage key, fixed decimal system (0 to 5 places) with automatic roundoff for dollar-and-cent answers. The unit features a credit balance indicator, leading zero suppression, and algebraic logic operation.

Measuring 3 x 5½ x 1¼ inches and weighs 9 ounces, its impact-resistant jewelry-style case will fit almost any shirt pocket or purse. **Columbia Scientific, 1730 22nd Street, Santa Monica, California 90404.**

her if she ever has any problems when it comes to converting ounces to cups, teaspoons to tablespoons, etc. She said she doesn't, but that she knows of some cooks who could use a little help. Therefore, it seems appropriate to include a few examples on typical conversions here for the majority of wives who are good cooks, but who could gain from a few kitchen conversion techniques.

Converting Teaspoons to Tablespoons.

Mrs. McKinley's American recipe calls for 8 ⅙ tbsp of salad oil, but she finds that for measuring she only has a teaspoon. How many teaspoons of salad oil should she use?

Mrs. McKinley solves her problem using the fact that there are 3 tsp in a tablespoon.

Procedure

Operation	Keyboard Entry	Function Touch	Display	Description
Set decimal to six places				
Clear registers and display		C	0.000000	
Enter fraction numerator	1	÷	1.000000	
Enter fraction denominator	6		0.166667	Fraction ⅙ in decimal form
Transfer display to add register	None	+	0.166667	
Enter whole part of salad oil measure	8	+	8.166667	Salad oil tablespoons in decimal form
Transfer display to multiply register	None	x	8.166667	
Enter conversion factor (U.S. tablespoons to U.S. teaspoons)	3	=	24.500001	Answer

Mrs. McKinley should use 24½ tsp of salad oil.

Converting Ounces of Weight to Fluid Ounces

How many fluid ounces of volume are occupied by water weighing 7½ oz?

To convert water from weight in ounces to volume in fluid ounces, multiply by the factor 1.0432.

Procedure

Operation	Keyboard Entry	Function Touch	Display	Description
Set decimal to four places				
Clear registers and display		C	0.0000	

Operation	Keyboard Entry	Function Touch	Display	Description
Enter water ounces from problem	7.5	÷	7.5000	
Enter conversion factor	1.0432	=	7.1894	Answer

Converting Fluid Ounces to Cups

How many cups are there in a 46 fl oz can of juice? There are 8 fl oz in a cup.

Procedure

Operation	Keyboard Entry	Function Touch	Display	Description
Set decimal to four places				
Clear registers and display		C	0.0000	
Enter volume (fluid ounces)	46	÷	46.0000	
Enter conversion factor (fluid ounces in a cup)	8	=	5.7500	Answer (record)

There are 5¾ cups in a 46 fl oz can of juice.

Word Problem in Converting U.S. Fluid Ounces to U.S. Cups

Mrs. Wilson has 106 fl oz of cottage cheese left to serve to 18 guests. If evenly divided, how many cups of cottage cheese will each guest receive? There are 8 ounces to a cup.

Procedure

Operation	Keyboard Entry	Function Touch	Display	Description
Set decimal to four places				
Clear registers and display		C	0.0000	
Enter volume (fluid ounces)	106	÷	106.0000	
Enter conversion factor (fluid ounces in a cup)	8	=	13.2500	Volume (cups)
Transfer display to divide register	None	÷	13.2500	
Enter number of guests	18	=	0.7361	Answer

Each guest will receive about ¾ cup of cottage cheese.

Word Problem in Converting Ounces to Cups

Mrs. Roosevelt's cook has 300 of the 10¾ oz cans of cream of chicken soup. The instructions on each can say to mix with 1 can of water. Mrs. Roosevelt's plan is to serve each guest 2 cups of soup, and she is planning to have 310 guests at the banquet. Should she buy more soup for the occasion?

One cup of canned cream of chicken soup weighs 8.6 oz before dilution.

Procedure

Operation	Keyboard Entry	Function Touch	Display	Description
Set decimal to four places				
Clear registers and display		C	0.0000	
Enter soup ounces in 1 can	10.75	÷	10.7500	
Enter soup ounces in 1 cup	8.6	=	1.2500	Can volume (cups)
Transfer display to multiply register	None	x	1.2500	
Enter dilution factor	2	=	2.5000	Cups of soup that can be made from 1 can
Transfer display to multiply register	None	x	2.5000	
Enter number of cans on hand	300	=	750.0000	Cups of soup that will be available from supplies on hand
Transfer display to divide register	None	÷	750.0000	
Enter number of cups per guest	2	=	375.0000	Number of guests who could be served with soup supply on hand

Since 375 guests could be served and only 310 guests are planned, the answer is that Mrs. Roosevelt will not need to buy more soup for this occasion.

Converting Ounces of Weight to Cups

How many cups of volume are occupied by 13⅛ oz of currants? There are 3⅜ cups of currants in a pound.

We must first convert 3⅜ to decimal form.

Procedure

Operation	Keyboard Entry	Function Touch	Display	Description
Set decimal to four places				
Clear registers and display		C	0.0000	
Enter fraction numerator	3		3.0000	
Enter fraction denominator	8		0.3750	Currant fraction in decimal form

Operation	Keyboard Entry	Function Touch	Display	Description
Transfer fraction to add register	None	+	0.3750	
Enter whole part of currant cups	3	+	3.3750	Conversion factor (cups per pound)
Transfer factor to dividend register	None		3.3750	
Enter number of ounces in a pound	16		0.2109	Conversion factor (cups per ounce)
Transfer display to multiply register	None	x	0.2109	
Enter currant ounces from problem	13.125		2.7681	Answer (record)

There are 13⅛ oz of currants in 2¾ cups.

Converting British Teaspoons to U.S. Tablespoons.

How many U.S. tablespoons are there in 6 British teaspoons? (There are 4.1634 British teaspoons in 1 U.S. tablespoon.)

How many U.S. tablespoons are there in 5 U.S. teaspoons? (There are 3 U.S. teaspoons in 1 U.S. tablespoon.)

How many U.S. tablespoons are there in 6⅞ U.S. teaspoons?

Procedure

Operation	Keyboard Entry	Function Touch	Display	Description
Set decimal to four places				
Clear registers and display		C	0.0000	
Enter first input (British teaspoons)	6	÷	6.0000	
Enter conversion factor (British teaspoons in U.S. tablespoon)	4.1634	=	1.4411	First answer (record)
Clear registers and display		C	0.0000	
Enter second input (U.S. teaspoons)	5	÷	5.0000	
Enter conversion factor (U.S. teaspoons in U.S. tablespoon)	3	=	1.6667	Second answer (record)
Clear registers and display		C	0.0000	
Enter third input numerator	7	÷	7.0000	
Enter third input denominator	8	=	0.8750	Third input fraction in decimal form

Operation	Keyboard Entry	Function Touch	Display	Description
Transfer display to add register	None	+	0.8750	
Enter third input integer	6	+	6.8750	Third input (U.S. teaspoons)
Transfer display to dividend register	None		6.8750	
Enter conversion factor (U.S. teaspoons in U.S. tablespoon)	3	=	2.2917	Third answer (record)

There are 1.44 U.S. tablespoons in 6 British teaspoons, 1.67 U.S. tablespoons in 5 U.S. teaspoons, and 2.29 U.S. tablespoons in 6⅞ U.S. teaspoons. In fractional units, these numbers approximate 1½, 1²/₃, and 2¼ U.S. teaspoons, respectively.

Converting British Fluid Ounces to U.S. Cups

How many U.S. cups of volume are occupied by 141 British fluid ounces of milk? (one U.S. cup is equal to 8.326748 British fluid ounces.)

Procedure

Operation	Keyboard Entry	Function Touch	Display	Description
Set decimal to four places				
Clear registers and display		C	0.0000	
Enter milk volume (British ounces)	141	÷	141.0000	
Enter conversion factor (British ounces in U.S. cup)	8.3267	=	16.9335	Answer (milk volume in U.S. cups)
Transfer display to subtract register	None	+	16.9335	
Enter whole number part	16	—	0.9335	Remainder (cups)
Transfer display to multiply register	None	x	0.9335	
Enter number of tablespoons in a cup (U.S.)	16	=	14.9360	Remainder (tablespoons)

We find that 141 British fluid ounces of milk occupy 16 cups 15 tbsp (U.S. measure).

Word Problem

Mrs. Taft has a British recipe from Wales calling for 92 British fluid ounces of nectarine juice. She wishes to ladle it

COMMODORE MINUTEMAN MODEL MM3-P—Measuring only 3 x 4 x 1 inch, the **Minuteman 3-P** lets you carry your calculator in your shirt pocket. A true four-function performer, with an 8-digit lighted display, it easily fits into the palm of your hand. The unit adds, subtracts, multiplies, and divides, does chain and mixed calculations, constant multiplication and division, true credit balance problems, and calculates percentages automatically with the operation of the percent key. The instrument also contains an accumulated discount key and a double cipher key.

The unit weighs only 5 ounces, and is available with disposable or rechargeable batteries (an ac adapter is optional). With most of the features of larger machines, at a much lower cost, the MM3-P provides maximum portability with a full keyboard designed for finger use. **Commodore Business Machines, Inc., 390 Reed Street, Santa Clara, California 95050.**

out of a punch bowl with a 1-cup ladle (U.S. measure). How many cups of nectarine juice should she use?

One U.S. cup is equal to 8.326748 British fluid ounces.

Procedure

Operation	Keyboard Entry	Function Touch	Display	Description
Set decimal to four places				
Clear registers and display		C	0.0000	
Enter volume (British fluid ounces)	92	÷	92.0000	
Enter conversion factor (British ounces in a U.S. cup)	8.3267	=	11.0488	Volume, U.S. cups (record)
Transfer display to subtract register	None	+	11.0488	
Enter whole-number part	11	−	0.0488	Remainder, U.S. cups
Transfer display to multiply register	None	x	0.0488	
Enter conversion factor (U.S. tablespoons in U.S. cups)	16	=	0.7808	Remainder, U.S. tbsp (record)

Mrs. Taft should ladle out 11 cups ¾ tbsp of nectarine juice (U.S. measure).

METRIC KITCHEN CONVERSIONS

We've touched upon some metric conversions already—converting metric recipes to U.S. measures. It is still good practice for the average housewife to become familiar with other metric conversion techniques in the kitchen. Being able to cook a few of those foreign delicacies will take you out of the category of average cooks and place you up with the superior cooks.

Converting Demiliters to Pints

Mrs. Hayes recipe for Pancakes Toulouse calls for 3 demiliters of buttermilk. How many pints in this? How many cups?

To convert demiliters to pints, we must multiply by the factor 1.0567. There are 2 cups to a pint.

Procedure

Operation	Keyboard Entry	Function	Display	Description
Set decimal to four places				
Clear registers and display		C	0.0000	

Operation	Keyboard Entry	Function Touch	Display	Description
Enter demiliters of buttermilk	3	x	3.0000	
Enter conversion factor (demiliters to U.S. pints)	1.0567	=	3.1701	U.S. pints
Transfer display to multiply register	None	x	3.1701	
Enter conversion factor (pints to cups)	2	=	6.3402	U.S. cups

Mrs. Hayes needs 6 ⅓ cups of buttermilk.

Converting Deciliters to Cups

Mrs. Garfield's recipe for crepes parisienne calls for 7 deciliters of milk. How many cups of milk does she need?
There are 0.4227 cups in one deciliter.

Procedure

Operation	Keyboard Entry	Function Touch	Display	Description
Set decimal to four places				
Clear registers and display		C	0.0000	
Enter milk deciliters	7	x	7.0000	
Enter conversion factor (deciliters to cups)	0.4227	=	2.9589	U.S. cups

Mrs. Garfield needs 3 cups of milk for her Parisian pancakes.

Converting Cubic Centimeters to Ounces

How many ounces do 65 cc (cubic centimeters) of seedless raisins weight?
One U.S. cup of seedless raisins weighs 5 ⅓ oz and occupies 236.5816 cc of volume.

Procedure

Operation	Keyboard Entry	Function Touch	Display	Description
Set decimal to four places				
Clear registers and display		C	0.0000	
Enter weight of one cup (ounces)	5.3333	÷	5.3333	
Enter volume of one cup (cc)	236.5816	=	0.0225	Density (ounces per cubic centimeter)

Operation	Keyboard Entry	Function Touch	Display	Description
Transfer display to multiply register	None	x	0.0225	
Enter volume from problem (cubic centimeters)	65	=	1.4653	Answer

The answer is that 65 cc of seedless raisins weigh about 1½ oz.

Converting Cubic Centimeters to Fluid Ounces

Odysseus Grant has 82 cc of semisweet chocolate. How many fluid ounces is this?

To convert cubic centimeters to fluid ounces, we must multiply the cubic centimeters by the factor 0.0338.

Procedure

Operation	Keyboard Entry	Function Touch	Display	Description
Set decimal to four places				
Clear registers and display		C	0.0000	
Enter cubic centimeters of chocolate	82	x	82.0000	
Enter conversion factor (cubic centimeters to U.S. fluid ounces)	.0338	=	2.7716	Answer

Odysseus has 2¾ fl oz of semisweet chocolate.

Simple Interest Calculators

This book has not been written for the professional accountant, who has many books of reference, semesters of education, and years of experience. To him, some of the examples given here are simple fundamentals, committed by him to memory long ago. His training and experience permit him to make interest calculations in his head; those of us who haven't such skills, however, find it much more convenient to employ an electronic calculator.

The basics of interest are presented here in such a manner as to clearly explain the "hows" and "whys" of such calculations. The chapter is designed to help one recognize the problem and know the procedure necessary to solve it. The problems illustrated and the solutions presented will greatly assist anyone in reaching an answer to any problem similar to the examples. By substituting the actual data into the example, and carrying out the calculations indicated, the answer will be obtained.

CONCEPTS OF INTEREST

Interest is the charge made for the use of borrowed money. The amount of the charge depends upon three factors: (1) the amount of money borrowed, (2) the length of time for which it is borrowed, and (3) the rate of interest. The amount borrowed is referred to as **principal**, and the rate of interest is a percentage of the principal. If a bank charged 8 percent interest, the charge for $100 borrowed for a full year would be $8.00.

Installment Loans

In practice, however, very few loans are made in which the entire principal is repaid in a lump sum at the end of a one-year period. Generally, loans are repaid a little each month, and each payment includes the interest charged for one month only. The amount of the payment in excess of the interest is applied to reduce the principal. This kind of loan is referred to as an **installment loan**, as it is repaid in installments. The interest charge must be calculated only for the number of days the principal is used, from one installment payment to the next. The principal balance is reduced each month, so it follows that the interest charge is also reduced each month. Interest charges are far greater in the early months of an installment loan than in the latter months when the principal balance becomes smaller.

If money is borrowed by month, as is sometimes the case, the interest charges are calculated at 1/12 of the annual interest rate. Thus, 6 percent interest per annum is equivalent to 1/2 percent per month.

Interest on Savings

When a deposit is made in a savings account, the institution receiving the funds, such as a bank, is in effect borrowing the money from the depositor. For the use of the depositor's funds, the institution pays him interest. Practically all of these institutions, including savings and loan associations, calculate interest on a daily basis, whether on investment money (deposits) or on loan fees. If it is **exact** interest, it is calculated daily at 1/365 of the annual interest. When ordinary interest calculations are used, the amount of the interest charges will be slightly greater than when exact interest calculations are used.

HOW IS INTEREST CALCULATED?

The basic method of computing simple interest is to multiply the principal amount times the annual interest rate, times the time the principal is used. The formula interest calculation is

$$\text{Principal} \times \text{Rate} \times \text{Time} = \text{Interest Charge}$$

Principal is expressed in exact dollars, rate is expressed as a decimal conversion of percentage, and time is usually (but not always) expressed on an annual basis. An interest rate of 8 percent is converted to the decimal 0.08. Five months of time is 5/12 (of a year), while 72 days is 72/360 in commercial calculations. In this book, when days are stated, the commercial practice will be followed.

Interest rates are often stated on a monthly basis. For example, many states allow **service** or **finance charges** equivalent to 1½ percent per month on the unpaid balance. If the unpaid balance amounted to $100, the service charge for one month would be 1½ percent of $100, or $1.50 (0.015 x $100).

PROMISSORY NOTES

Commercial loans may be obtained from several sources, but in almost every case the one receiving the loan must sign a formal document called a **promissory note.** Such an instrument signed by the debtor is evidence that a loan was in fact granted, in case court action is ever required. Most promissory notes are transferrable, so that the holder may sell a note to another for cash or in settlement of another obligation. Promissory notes are usually referred to as **notes,** and can either be **demand** notes, or **term** notes. A demand note can be "called" (made due) at any time by the one holding the note, while a term note becomes due only on the terms specified in the instrument.

Maturity

An interst-bearing note provides for interest charges from the date of issuance to the due date, or **maturity.** It is customary for banks and other lending institutions to agree to lend money for certain specified periods of time. A note that is due 90 days after issuance is referred to as a 90-day note. Ninety days after issuance, the principal and accrued interest of the note are payable. Notes with due dates later than 1 year usually require interest to be paid at definite intervals, such as quarterly or semiannually. A note may, according to its terms, mature 3 months from the date of issuance, as opposed to 90 days. In this event, interest charges are usually calculated on a monthly (rather than number of day) basis, and the note is due exactly 3 months from the date issued. A note issued on July 3 and due in 3 months would be payable on October 3, even though a total of 92 days has elapsed.

Mortgage Note

A **mortgage note** is a promissory note secured by certain property, such as land, buildings, and equipment. If the debtor is unable to pay the note when due, the creditor has a legal claim on the property mortgaged. Ordinarily, when one speaks of his mortgage, he is referring to a promissory note secured by his real property, although anything of value can be mortgaged—furniture, automobiles, equipment, etc. Mortgage notes are similar to other notes, calling for a certain amount of interest and principal payments at specified intervals.

TRUTH IN LENDING

Title I of the Consumer Credit Protection Act has been in effect since July 1, 1969. Anyone that extends credit to consumers—whether the transaction involves merchandise, services, or a loan—is affected by this legislation if any finance charge is or may be payable, or if the credit is repayable in more than four installments. The Board of Governors of the Federal Reserve System have issued a set of rules known as Regulation Z, the purpose of which is to require lenders to inform borrowers and credit customers of the exact cost of credit so that these costs can be compared to other sources of credit.

The **finance charge** and the **annual percentage rate** are really the two most important disclosures required by this regulation. If these disclosures are not made, the consumer may sue for twice the amount of the finance charge (limited to a minimum of $100 and a maximum of $1000), plus costs and attorney's fees. Any installment contract consummated after July 1, 1969 must disclose the annual percentage rate. To perform any kind of interest calculations on the electronic calculator, it is desirable that the interest rate regarding that particular contract be known. Obviously, the source of that information is the Regulation Z disclosure statement.

ADD-ON INTEREST

As simple as **add-on interest** sounds, it is not simple interest, it is nevertheless important to mention add-on interest; at this point. If an installment loan of $1000 is made at an add-on interest rate of 8 percent for a term of 3 years, interest is precalculated and added to the principal amount of the loan. In this example, the interest is calculated at the rate times the number of years to arrive at the add-on interest over the full 3-year period (0.08 x 3=0.24=24 percent). Twenty-four percent of $1000 is $240. The installment note is made out for $1240, and this is typically divided into 36 monthly payments.

With simple interest, the amount of interest due each month is based on the amount of the principal at the time the payment is made. On an installment loan, the principal is reduced each time a payment is made, so the amount of interest paid on each installment is also reduced on each successive payment. Eight-percent simple interest is far less expensive than 8 percent add-on interest.

As an illustration of the difference between the cost of add-on interest and simple interest, we have determined that in the example given above, 8-percent add-on interest on an installment loan of $1000 for a term of 3 years is $240. This same installment loan at 8 percent **simple** interest would call for an interest charge of only $128.10! Using tables prepared by the U.S. Government, we find that 8 percent add-on interest over a 3-year period on a $1000 loan is actually 14.5 percent simple interest.

Whether simple interest or add-on interest is charged, the charges are calculated in advance, when the loan papers are prepared, as required in the Truth In Lending Law. The finance charge is then added to the principal, and the total is divided by the number of months installment payments are to be made. The result is the amount of each monthly payment.

SIMPLE INTEREST VERSUS COMPOUND INTEREST

The exercises in this chapter deal only with **simple** interest. However, it should be noted that banks and savings institutions usually compensate their depositors on a **compound** interest basis. This means that the interest is calculated periodically and added to the principal amount. The new principal amount is then used for the calculation of interest at the end of the next succeeding period. The length of these periods varies with the various institutions, from as little as one day to as much as one year. The shorter the period, the better it is for the depositor, because his principal increases at a faster rate, and therefore the amount of interest he receives also increases at a faster rate. **Simple** interest calculations, however, do not take into consideration the fact that interest may be paid and added to the principal sometime during the period in question. If interest were paid during the period, and added to the principal, the interest earned would not be simple, but would be called **compound interest.**

INTEREST FORMULAS

The basic formula for computing simple interest is

Principal x Rate x Time = Interest charge

We will let P stand for principal expressed in dollars, R stand for rate of interest expressed as a decimal, T stand for time in years, and I stand for interest charge. Thus, the above 'formula becomes

$$PRT = I$$

We are able to calculate the value of any one of the factors in this equation if the other three factors are known. To calculate the values of the other factors, we must rearrange the formula slightly. For example, to calculate principal, the formula becomes

$$P = I / RT$$

To calculate rate of interest, the formula becomes

$$R = I / PT$$

To calculate the time, the formula becomes

$$T = I / PR$$

Now, no matter what type of simple interest problem is presented to us, we are able to just substitute the known value, carry out the indicated calculations, and solve the problem.

SOLVING FOR AMOUNT OF INTEREST

Before attempting to solve any of the examples given in this chapter, it is important that the reader review the introductory material in this chapter. We have avoided the use of formulas and equations where possible, but in the interest of conserving space, we have adopted the use of the basic formula for calculating interest. The exercises that follow will use the formula, $I = P \times R \times T$.

Annual Interest

What is the annual simple interest on $62 at the rate of 4½ percent?

In the problem, $P = \$62$, $R = 4½$, and $T = 1$. We can ignore T in our calculation, since 1 times any number equals that number.

Procedure

Operation	Keyboard Entry	Function Touch	Display	Description
Set decimal to four places				
Clear registers and display		C	0.0000	
Enter principal	62	x	62.0000	
Enter interest rate expressed as a decimal	.045	=	2.7900	Answer

The annual simple interest on $62 at 4½ percent is $2.79.

Seven-Year Interest

What is the amount of simple interest on $834 for 7 years at 6 percent?

The formula to be used here is

$$I = RTP$$

In the problem, $R = 6$ percent, $T = 7$ years, and $P = \$834$.

Procedure

Operation	Keyboard Entry	Function Touch	Display	Description
Set decimal to three places				
Clear registers and display		C	0.000	
Enter interest rate expressed as a decimal	.06	x	0.060	
Enter principal	834	=	50.04	1 year's simple interest (dollars)
Transfer display to multiply register	None	x	50.04	
Enter time	7	=	350.28	Answer

The simple interest on $834 for 7 years at 6 percent is $350.28.

Ordinary Simple Interest Between Two Dates

What is the ordinary simple interest on $246 at 8.9 percent from April 8, 1973, to November 1, 1973?

The formula for ordinary simple interest for a period of days is

$$\text{Ordinary Simple Interest} = \frac{\text{Principal x Interest Rate x Time}}{360}$$

Procedure

Operation	Keyboard Entry	Function Touch	Display	Description
Set decimal to five places				
Clear registers and display		C	0.00000	
Enter days in a month (ordinary)	30	+	30.00000	
Enter first day number (April 8, 1973)	8	−	22.00000	Days to be counted in April (record)
Clear registers and display		C	0.00000	
Enter months from May through October, inclusive	6	x	6.00000	
Enter days in a month	30	=	180.00000	Days in May through October, inclusive
Transfer display to add register	None	+	180.00000	
Enter days to be counted in April	22	+	202.00000	Days from April 8 through end of October
Enter days to be counted in November	1	+	203.00000	

Operation	Keyboard Entry	Function Touch	Display	Description
Transfer display to dividend register	None	÷	203.00000	Time (days)
Enter denominator (ordinary days in a year)	360	=	0.56389	Time (years)
Transfer display to multiply register	None	x	0.56389	
Enter principal (dollars)	246	=	138.71694	Principal multiplied by time
Transfer display to multiply register	None	x	138.71694	
Enter interest rate (decimal form of 8.9 percent)	.089	=	12.34581	Answer

The ordinary simple interest on $246 at 8.9 percent from April 8, 1973, to November 1, 1973 is $12.35.

Ordinary Simple Interest

What is the ordinary simple interest on $7500 at 8½ percent for 7 weeks?

The equation for ordinary simple interest with time in weeks is

$$\text{Ordinary Simple Interest} = \frac{\text{Principal x Interest Rate x Time}}{52}$$

Procedure

Operation	Keyboard Entry	Function Touch	Display	Description
Set decimal to four places				
Clear registers and display		C	0.0000	
Enter principal (dollars)	7500	x	7500.0000	
Enter interest rate (decimal form of 8 1/2 percent)	.085	=	637.5000	
Transfer display to multiply register	None	x	637.5000	Annual interest
Enter time (weeks)	7	=	4462.5000	Numerator
Transfer display to divide register	None	÷	4462.5000	
Enter denominator (ordinary weeks in a year)	52	=	85.8173	Answer

The ordinary simple interest on $7500 at 8½ percent for 7 weeks is $85.82.

COLUMBIA "MEMORY II" MODEL—The **Memory II**, priced under $100, performs the four basic math operations, but features a memory that can be used for constant multiplication, division, addition, or subtractions. A lightweight, at only 6½ ounces, the unit measures 3 x 5½ x ⅞ inches, making it convenient for pocket or purse.

The calculator has an 8-digit LED display and completely rechargeable batteries. An ac adapter for 110V operation can be employed. It uses algebraic logic, and has a combination floating-fixed decimal system (fixed at 0 to 5 places), with automatic roundoff. The memory key can be used for retaining totals, and the overflow-underflow indicator prevents errors. The keyboard features silent, deep-throw operation. **Columbia Scientific, 1730 22nd Street, Santa Monica, California 90404.**

Monthly Interest

John has a loan balance of $541, which is payable monthly. He knows that he is paying 10 percent annual interest. How much interest will he pay on his next monthly installment?

Loan balances are reduced each time an installment payment is made, but we can take 10 percent of $541 and divide that by 12 to determine the interest this month. The interest charge the following month will be a different amount, because with installment loans, the principal balance is reduced each month.

Procedure

Operation	Keyboard Entry	Function Touch	Display	Description
Set decimal to five places				
Clear registers and display		C	0.00000	
Enter loan balance	541	x	541.00000	
Enter percent interest (expressed as a decimal)	.10	=		
Transfer display to divide register	None	÷	54.10000	
Enter number of months in one year	12	=	4.50833	Answer

John will pay $4.51 in interest charges on his next monthly installment.

90-Day Loan

In three months, a bond that Fred has will mature, and he will receive $3500. He planned to buy a particular truck with the $3500, but he has found one now that is on sale for $2500—a savings of $1000 if he buys immediately. The bank agrees to lend $2500 to Fred for 90 days at an annual interest rate of 7 percent. Fred knows he will have to pay interest, but on the other hand, he will be saving $1000 on the truck purchase. What is the net amount that Fred will save as a result of the two transactions?

The formula we will use to calculate the interest is

$$I = PRT$$

Once we know the interest, we will subtract that amount from $1000 to arrive at the net savings.

Procedure

Operation	Keyboard Entry	Function Touch	Display	Description
Set decimal to four places				
Clear registers and display		C	0.0000	
Enter time (days)	90	÷	90.0000	
Enter conversion factor (ordinary days in a year)	360	=	0.2500	Time in years
Transfer display to multiply register	None	x	0.2500	
Enter principal (dollars)	2500	=	625.0000	Principal multiplied by time
Transfer display to multiply register	None	x	625.0000	
Enter interest rate (7 percent expressed as a decimal number)	.07	=	43.7500	Interest cost of bank loan (record)
Clear registers and display		C	0.0000	
Enter saving on purchase (dollars)	1000	+	1000.0000	
Enter cost of loan (dollars)	43.75	—	956.2500	Net gain

Fred is ahead $956.25 on the two transactions.

Savings Account Interest

A customer deposited $6000 in a bank, 6 years and 4 months ago. The bank agreed to pay him simple interest at the rate of 4¾ percent per year. What is the amount of interest earned?

The formula for this problem is

$$I = P \times R \times T$$

P is $6000, R is 0.0475 (4¾ percent expressed as a decimal), and T is 6 years and 4 months.

Procedure

Operation	Keyboard Entry	Function Touch	Display	Description
Set decimal to four places				
Clear registers and display		C	0.0000	
Enter months part of time	4	÷	4.0000	
Enter conversion factor (months in a year)	12	=	0.3333	

Operation	Keyboard Entry	Function Touch	Display	Description
Transfer display to add register	None	+	0.3333	Four months expressed in terms of a year
Enter years part of time	6	+	6.3333	Time in decimal form (record)
Clear registers and display		C	0.0000	
Enter principal (dollars)	6000	x	6000.0000	
Enter interest rate (per year)	.0475	=	285.0000	Amount of interest per year
Transfer display to multiply register	None	x	285.0000	
Enter time (in decimal form)	6.3333	=	1804.9905	Answer

The simple interest on $6000 for 6 years and 4 months at 4¾ percent is $1804.99.

Finding Combined Interest and Principle

Adam inherited his grandfather's savings account. He found that his grandfather had deposited $7500 in the account 11 years ago at 4¾ percent simple interest. Including the accrued interest and the principal, how much did Adam inherit?

In this problem, we must first calculate the interest amount, and then add this amount to the principal. The formulas we will use are

$$I = PRT$$

$$\text{Total Inheritance} = I + P$$

Procedure

Operation	Keyboard Entry	Function Touch	Display	Description
Set decimal to four places				
Clear registers and display		C	0.0000	
Enter time (years)	11	x	11.0000	
Enter interest rate (4-3—4 percent in decimal form)	.0475	=	0.5225	
Transfer display to multiply register	None	x	0.5225	
Enter principal (dollars)	7500	=	3918.7500	Total interest
Reset decimal to two places				
Clear registers and display		C	0.00	
Enter principal (dollars)	7500	+	7500.00	
Enter simple interest (dollars)	3918.75	+	11418.75	Total interest plus principal

Adam inherited $11,418.75.

SOLVING FOR PRINCIPAL

Suppose your mother asks you to find out how much money she has in her savings account. She has forgotten the principal amount; however, she knows that the bank pays her 5 percent interest, and her last annual interest check was $312.40. What is the amount on deposit?

It is not necessary to contact the bank. There is enough information here to calculate the principal on the electronic calculator. We will use the formula

$$P = I/RT$$

where I = $312.50, R = 5 percent, and T = 1.

Procedure

Operation	Keyboard Entry	Function Touch	Display	Description
Set decimal to four places				
Clear registers and display		C	0.0000	
Enter amount of interest check	312.40	÷	312.4000	
Enter interest rate (expressed as a decimal)	.05	=	6248.0000	Answer

Calculating Original Deposit

Geronimo made a deposit in the Pancho Villa Bank in Chihuahua in 1922 and left it there at a simple interest rate of 3 percent until 1973, when his heirs were made aware of the deposit. The interest that had accrued was 80,000 reales. What was Geronimo's original deposit?

Referring to our interest formulas in the beginning of this chapter, we find that to solve for the principal, we must use the formula

$$P = I / RT$$

where I = 80,000 reales, R = 3 percent, and T = 51 years (1973—1922)

Procedure

Operation	Keyboard Entry	Function Touch	Display	Description
Clear registers and display		C	0.000	
Enter rate of interest (expressed as a decimal)	.03	x	0.030	
Enter time in years	51	=	1.530	Denominator in formula (record)

Operation	Keyboard Entry	Function Touch	Display	Description
Clear registers and display		C	0.000	
Enter interest amount	80000	÷	80000.000	
Enter denominator (from above calculation)	1.53	=	52287.581	Answer

Geronimo's original deposit was 52,287.58 reales (pronounced "ray-ALL-ace").

SOLVING FOR RATE OF INTEREST

The bank will make a construction loan in the amount of $5525 on a 90-day note. At the end of the 90 days, the bank must be repaid a total of $5635.50. What is the rate of interest that the bank charges?

The formula we must use here is

$$R = I / PT$$

where I equals the difference between the amount borrowed and the amount repaid; P is $5525; and T is $^{90}/_{360}$, or one-fourth of a year.

Procedure

Operation	Keyboard Entry	Function Touch	Display	Description
Set decimal to four places				
Clear registers and display		C	0.0000	
Enter amount to be repaid	5635.50	+	5635.5000	
Enter original loan amount	5525	—	110.5000	Amount of interest charged by bank
Transfer display to divide register	None	÷	110.5000	I
Enter principal amount, P	5525	÷	0.0200	
Enter T (1/4, expressed as a decimal)	.25	=	0.0800	Answer, expressed as a decimal

The interest rate being charged by the bank is 0.08, or 8 percent.

Rate of Interest Problem

Eight months ago, Filbert borrowed $280 from an acquaintance; now he owes that amount, plus accrued interest of $18. What interest rate is he paying?

To solve for the interest rate, we use the formula

$$R = I / PT$$

where I=$18, P=$280, and T=8 mo.

Procedure

Operation	Keyboard Entry	Function Touch	Display	Description
Set decimal to four places				
Clear registers and display		C	0.0000	
Enter amount of interest	18	÷	18.0000	
Enter principal	280	÷	0.0642	
Enter time as part of a year (2/3 as a decimal)	.6667	x	0.0962	
Multiply by 100 for percent conversion	100		9.6200	Answer

Filbert is paying 9.62 percent interest.

SOLVING FOR TIME

Assume that you have $700 in the bank, in a savings account. You do not wish to use any of the $700 principal, but there is something you wish to purchase, which costs $38.50. You decide to use the interest you will accumulate on your savings account. If the bank is paying 6 percent interest on your savings, how long will it take to accumulate $38.50 in interest?

The unknown in this exercise is time, so we will use the formula

$$T = I / PR$$

where R = 6 percent, P = $700, and I = $38.50. We can tell by examining the problem that it will take less than one year to earn the required amount of interest, since $700 at 7 percent for one year will yield $49. Therefore, let us look for the time in months, instead of years. To do this, we simply determine the rate of interest per month and substitute that rate in the formula. All other factors remain the same.

Procedure

Operation	Keyboard Entry	Function Touch	Display	Description
Set decimal to five places				
Clear registers and display		C	0.00000	
Enter rate of interest per year (in decimal form)	.06	÷	0.06000	

Operation	Keyboard Entry	Function Touch	Display	Description
Enter number of months in 1 year	12	=	0.00500	Rate of interest per month
Transfer display to multiply register	None	x	0.00500	
Enter principal amount	700	=	3.50000	Amount of interest per month (record)
Clear registers and display		C	0.00000	
Enter total interest desired	38.50	÷	38.50000	
Enter interest earnings per month	3.50	=	11.00000	Answer

It will take 11 months to accumulate $38.50 interest.

Converting Interest to Time

Ralph borrowed $4418 from the bank on a 180-day note, at a rate of interest of 8 percent. He paid the note before the 180 days passed, and the bank charged him interest of $117.81. How long did he use the money?

The unknown in this example is time, so we will use the formula

$$T = I / PR$$

where $I = \$117.81$, $P = \$4418$, and $R = 8$ percent.

Since we are dealing with a period of less than 1 year, it would be appropriate to determine the interest rate per month, and then substitute that rate in place of 8 percent. The solution is then expressed in months, rather than as a decimal portion of a year.

Procedure

Operation	Keyboard Entry	Function Touch	Display	Description
Set decimal to four places				
Clear registers and display		C	0.0000	
Enter annual interest rate (expressed as a decimal)	.08	÷	0.0800	
Enter months in a year	12	=	0.0066	Interest rate per month (record)
Clear registers and display		C	0.0000	
Enter interest charge	117.81	÷	117.8100	
Enter principal	4418	÷	0.0266	
Enter interest rate per month	.0066	=	4.0303	

Ralph used the bank's money for approximately 4 months.

Income Tax Preparation

Each year, I am faced with what I regard as a most unpleasant task—preparing my federal income tax return. I usually do a lot of worrying about it until, on April 14th, I finally compile all the figures, do the necessary mathematical calculations, and fill out the forms. The next day, blurry eyed from lack of sleep, I tell my friends what an easy time I had in filling out my tax forms. But I know that this year will be a lot easier—thanks to my electronic calculator. I used to spend a lot of time figuring, checking, rechecking, etc. Now I know that I won't have to spend nearly as much time at those laborious calculations. Don't get me wrong. I'm certainly not looking forward to income tax time. But I don't cringe when I think about it any more.

If we are wage earners, that is, if we draw a salary from an employer, we pay toward our income tax by way of withholding tax. Otherwise, we send in quarterly payments with a declaration of estimated tax. Either way, we must keep records, and then, using those records, enter certain information on the tax return forms provided by Uncle Sam. It is the correct entry of that information on the forms that is of utmost concern to us. We find that in order to enter the information required, we must be able to perform a variety of mathematical operations.

We must report our gross income from all sources, list our dependents, prepare our schedule of deductions—and seemingly list ten thousand other details about our private lives. Then we must manipulate the data in various ways and place totals, subtotals, tax calculations, etc. in the little blocks provided on the form. No matter what the politicians say, the forms seem a bit more complicated each year—not to mention the tax laws themselves. By the time some vague tax law is clarified in the courts, Congress changes it. We can't win! So, let's make the best of it, and from now on, simplify the work ourselves with our electronic wizard.

HERMES MODEL 320—The 320 is a desk-type electronic printing calculator with a capacity of 15 digits plus 2 symbols. The manufacturer claims that the keyboard has been scientifically designed by placing the function keys used most frequently within easy reach of the home keys, and by individually shaping the keys so that the fingers will not accidentally slide all over the keyboard. The 320 prints large, easy-to-read numbers each time a function key is touched, so that a permanent record is made of the input and the result. The unit is silent except for the sound of the printer. An interesting feature of the calculator is its drop-in ribbon cassette, which eliminates smudged fingers or service calls for ribbon replacement.

The 320 has a dual decimal system that features a floating-in/fixed-out decimal as well as add mode (in any decimal setting), and the programed percent key makes figuring markups, discounts, and new balances easy. In addition to the four basic mathematical functions, the unit will automatically recall the last printed number without reentry. In credit balance calculations, the negative numbers will print in red. A full floating decimal system (0-15 places) can be used for entry of multiplication and division factors, or the preset decimal system (0-8 places) can be used for all modes. The dual decimal system can be set either to accept whole numbers or automatically position the decimal point where preset (add-mode). The 320 also features automatic constant, direct chain multiplication and division, and direct accumulation of products and quotients. It will automatically drop and round off products and quotients. **Paillard Incorporated, 1900 Lower Rd., Linden, N.J. 07036.**

In this chapter, we are going to take a close look at some of the common calculations we are required to make each year. You and I will be able to spend a lot less time on our tax return this year, thanks to electronics.

DATA REQUIRED

Before we begin filling out the tax forms, we should have all of the information pertaining to our gross income, our deductions from gross income, our other itemized deductions, and our personal exemptions. **Gross income** is all of our income from any source, including wages and interest received. The deductions from gross income include trade and business deductions not incurred as an employee; also travel expenses, including cost of meals and lodging, which you incurred while you were away from home on business for your employer. Itemized deductions are those items such as contributions; interest expenses; taxes; medical expenses, including drugs; and miscellaneous other deductions such as uniforms, tools, union dues, employment agency fees, etc. Personal exemptions are those allowed for ourselves, our spouses, our children, and certain other dependents.

GENERAL PROCEDURE FOR FIGURING YOUR TAX

The first thing to do is add up your gross income, including the gross income of your spouse if you are filing a joint return. Ordinarily, there is a tax savings if a joint return is filed. Next, you must identify the deductions from gross income to arrive at the **adjusted gross income.** These deductions generally pertain to business-related deductions such as trade deductions, certain transportation expenses, outside salesmen's expenses, losses from sale of property, etc. Moving expenses and certain other expenses are also deductible from gross income. Once we have determined all of the deductions from gross income, we are ready to move to step 3.

Carefully review all of your records—canceled checks, receipts, and memory—and list contributions, interest expense, medical expenses, taxes, and other miscellaneous items allowed. This is your schedule A itemized deductions. Perform the necessary calculations, and compare the total with the standard deduction. You will want to use whichever gives you the greater deduction.

In step 4, simply determine the deduction Uncle Sam gives you for personal exemptions (yourself, spouse, children, and certain other people you support). For step 5, add your deductions from Schedule A (or your standard deduction, if that is larger) to the personal exemption deduction. Next (step 6), subtract that total from the adjusted gross income to arrive at your **taxable income**. The seventh step is to calculate the tax by using the proper tax rate schedule. Finally, for step 8, subtract all credits from the amount of tax calculated in step 7. These credits include taxes withheld from wages, prepaid estimated taxes, overpayment of social security taxes, and other items.

PURPOSE OF THIS CHAPTER

You are cautioned not to use this chapter as a guide for the preparation of your federal income tax return. The purpose of this chapter is solely to demonstrate how you can use the electronic calculator to aid in performing the mathematical operations necessary in the return. The names we have used here are fictitious, and the rates used in the examples are subject to change by congressional action. We suggest you contact your local Internal Revenue Service office for a copy of a very helpful book for individuals to use in the preparation of their federal income tax return. The book, which sells for less than $1, is also available from the Superintendent of Documents, Washington, D.C. 20402.

GROSS INCOME

The Government defines gross income as income that is subject to tax. This really doesn't tell us a whole lot, but gross income is that received for services performed (wages); business income; profit from sale of property; rent; interest; dividends; and gains, profits, or income derived from any source whatsoever, unless exempt from tax by law. To the ordinary working man, all income is taxable, it seems. Items to be included in gross income are compensation for services (before payroll deductions), commissions, interest on savings, back pay, tips, bonuses, awards and prizes, etc. A gift is nontaxable.

The following example illustrates how gross income can be computed using the electronic calculator.

Calculating Gross Income

George Lincoln received $10,100 in wages and a $100 bonus, $813 commission from the sale of property, $27 interest on his savings account, and new winnings of $433 from gambling in Las Vegas. He received no other income. His wife received $75 from a short story she sold to a magazine. What will be the total gross income shown on their joint return?

Procedure

Operation	Keyboard Entry	Function Touch	Display	Description
Set decimal to zero places				
Clear registers and display		C	0	
Enter wages	10100	+	10100	
Enter bonus	100	+	10200	Running total
Enter commission	813	+	11013	Running total
Enter interest	27	+	11040	Running total
Enter net winnings	433	+	11473	Running total
Enter wife's earnings	75	+	11548	Gross income

George Lincoln and his wife will show a gross income of $11,548 on their joint return.

DEDUCTIONS FROM GROSS INCOME

To be deductible from gross income, an expense must be "ordinary and necessary" in carrying on any trade, business, or profession. It can be a nonbusiness expense, but it must be incurred in pursuit of the collection or production of income (including the collection or refund of any tax) or incurred in the management, conservation, or maintenance of property held for income purposes. Some of the business expenses that are deductible are: costs of supplies, rent, traveling, entertainment, advertising, operation of an automobile, cost of labor, insurance premiums, etc. Fines are not considered a business deduction. If you are required to work at home as a condition of your employment, you can deduct a reasonable share of depreciation or rent, maintenance, and other housing expenses.

In the following example, the employee was obligated to make a business trip for his employer.

Business Trip Deduction

Ralph Wall is calculating his deductions from gross income. In looking over his records, he finds that he took a business trip for his employer and paid the expenses himself. His airfare was $276, his food and lodging while he was on the trip was $212, and the other expenses of the trip came to $42. During the year, he also incurred expenses of $408 while he was an outside salesman. What are his total deductions from gross income?

189

Procedure

Operation	Keyboard Entry	Function Touch	Display	Description
Set decimal to zero places				
Clear registers and display		C	0	
Enter airfare	276			
		+	276	
Enter food and lodging	212			
		+	488	Running total
Enter other business expenses	42			
		+	530	Running total
Enter outside sales-man's expenses	408			
		+	938	Answer

Ralph Wall may deduct $938 from his gross income.

CALCULATION OF ADJUSTED GROSS INCOME

The adjusted gross income figure controls the limit on the child care deduction, the amount of the standard and medical deductions, the charitable contribution deduction limit, the use of the tax tables, and the amount of tax from the tax tables. It is important to include all allowable items in the deductions from gross income to arrive at the lowest adjusted gross income figure permissible, since the lower the adjusted gross income figure, the better it is for the taxpayer.

To arrive at the adjusted gross income figure, it is necessary to subtract the deductions from gross income from the gross income figure.

Adjusted Gross Income

John Stone has a gross income of $12,446, and deductions from gross income of $789. What is his adjusted gross income?

Procedure

Operation	Keyboard Entry	Function Touch	Display	Description
Set decimal to zero places				
Clear registers and display		C	0	
Enter gross income	12446	+	12446	
Enter deductions	789	−	11657	

John Stone's adjusted gross income is $11,657.

PERSONAL EXEMPTIONS

You can take a personal exemption for yourself, your spouse, your dependent children, and certain other individuals who are dependent upon you for support. There are certain requirements and limitations, so it would be wise to carefully review the law before taking a questionable exemption. You are allowed an extra exemption if you are over 65; and if you are blind, the law allows another extra exemption. The same applies to your spouse, if you are filing a joint return.

Personal Exemptions Example

Tom Smith has a wife and three children. He and his wife are both under 65, and both have good vision. He is the sole support for the three children, and he is entitled to an exemption for the children and his wife. If he and his wife file a joint return, and the exemptions allowed by law for the year in question are $750 each, what will be the amount of his personal exemptions?

There are five members of the family entitled to an exemption.

Procedure

Operation	Keyboard Entry	Function Touch	Display	Description
Set decimal to zero places				
Clear registers and display		C	0	
Enter number of exemptions	5	x	5	
Enter amount allowed for each exemption	750	=	3750	Answer

Tom Smith will enter $3750 for his personal exemptions.

DEDUCTION FOR MEDICAL EXPENSES

If you itemize your deductions, you are entitled to deduct the medical expenses you pay for yourself, your spouse, and your dependents. The expenses must exceed a certain portion of your adjusted gross income, and can be fees paid to physicians, dentists, surgeons, eye doctors, authorized Christian Scientist practitioners, practical or registered nurses, qualified psychologists, chiropractors, osteopaths, etc. Laboratory and hospital costs, medicine, drugs, special aids and supplies, and similar expenses are deductible.

The following example illustrates how Mr. Bane calculated his medical deduction.

Calculating Medical Deductions

Timothy Bane has an adjusted gross income of $8832. In adding up his yearly medical expenses, he finds he has paid $129 for prescriptions and drugs, $78 to Waldo Hospital, $190 to

Dr. White, $92 to Dr. Black, $55 to Dr. Brown, and $22 to Dr. Green. What amount is he allowed for the medical expense deduction?

When Mr. Bane prepared his tax return, the tax law in effect stated that medical expenses are deductible only to the extent they exceed 3 percent of his adjusted gross income. His medical expenses can include only the portion of his prescription and drug expense that exceeds 1 percent of his adjusted gross income.

Procedure

Operation	Keyboard Entry	Function Touch	Display	Description
Set decimal to three places				
Clear registers and display		C	0.000	
Enter gross income	8832	x	8832.000	
Enter 1 percent as a decimal	.01	=	88.320	1 percent of adjusted gross income (record)
Transfer display to multiply register	None	x	88.320	
Enter 3 (3 times 1 percent give 3 percent)	3	=	264.960	3 percent of adjusted gross income (record)
Clear registers and display		C	0.000	
Enter medicine costs	129	+	129.000	
Enter 1 percent of adjusted gross income	88.32	—	40.680	Allowed deduction for medicine costs
Enter hospital costs	78	+	118.680	Running total
Enter Dr. White's charges	190	+	308.680	Running total
Enter Dr. Black's charges	92	+	400.680	Running total
Enter Dr. Brown's charges	55	+	455.680	Running total
Enter Dr. Green's charges	22	+	477.680	Running total
Enter 3 percent of adjusted gross income	264.96	—	212.720	Allowed deduction

Timothy Bane is allowed $212.72 as a medical expense deduction.

DEDUCTION FOR CONTRIBUTIONS

Many organizations require contributions if they are to remain in operation. You may deduct your contributions to qualified organizations if you itemize your deductions, and if the contributions do not exceed a certain limit.

SHARP MODEL EL-805—The biggest factor in battery life in an elec
tronic calculator is the display. The engineers at Sharp have taken advantage of a newly developed liquid-crystal display which consumes very
little energy and prolongs battery life considerably. Although the display
is not as bright as in some models, one inexpensive ordinary dry cell
battery will provide over 100 hours of continuous use. Since the EL-805 is
so economical to operate, an ac adapter or battery charging unit is not
necessary.

The instrument has an 8-digit display and capacity with a zero suppression system (unnecessary zeros are not displayed). It features a
complete floating decimal system, a minus-sign indicator, a constant-
mode indicator, and repeat addition and subtraction. The EL-805 will
perform the four basic arithmetic calculations, chain multiplication and
division, constant multiplication and division, power calculations, tax
calculations, and mixed calculations. It has an automatic clearing
system.

The unit measures 3⅛ x 4¾ x 1¼ inches, and weighs a little over 7
ounces. **Sharp Electronics Corporation, 10 Keystone Place, Paramus,
New Jersey 07652.**

Contributions Example

George Brown made contributions to the First Baptist Church in the amount of $520, Boy Scouts of America in the amount of $75, and the Red Cross in the amount of $104. He made other contributions to miscellaneous organized charities in the amount of $24. What is his deduction for contributions?

Procedure

Operation	Keyboard Entry	Function Touch	Display	Description
Set decimal to zero places				
Clear registers and display		C	0	
Enter church contribution	520	+	520	
Enter Boy Scouts contribution	75	+	595	Running total
Enter Red Cross contribution	104	+	699	Running total
Enter miscellaneous contributions	24	+	723	Total

George Brown may deduct $723 for contributions.

DEDUCTION FOR INTEREST EXPENSE

If you itemize your deductions, you may deduct interest paid on your indebtedness. One of the biggest interest items is the home mortgage, but other large interest items are installment loans and bank notes. Usually, at the end of each year, it is possible to contact the various lenders for information regarding the amount of interest you paid during the year.

Interest Expense Example

Joan Westgate paid interest on several installment accounts as follows: Jack's Department Store, $17.50; Second National Bank, $313.12; App's Appliance Stores, $55.00, and Spinnin' Wheels Bicycle Shop, $12.25. What is her deduction for interest expense?

Procedure

Operation	Keyboard Entry	Function Touch	Display	Description
Set decimal to two places				
Clear registers and display		C	0.00	
Enter interest paid to Jack's Department Store	17.50	+	17.50	
Enter interest paid to Second National Bank	313.12	+	330.62	Running total

Operation	Keyboard Entry	Function Touch	Display	Description
Enter interest paid to App's Appliance Store	55.00	+	385.620	Running total
Enter interest paid to Spinnin' Wheels Shop	12.25	+	397.870	Total

Joan Westgate can deduct $397.87 as her interest expense.

DEDUCTION FOR TAXES

The Internal Revenue Code provides for deduction of some state, local, and foreign taxes, such as property taxes, state income taxes, certain local taxes, sales and use taxes, state gasoline taxes, etc.

Deduction for Taxes Example

George Lincoln found that he had paid $740 in property taxes, $115 in sales taxes, $190 in gasoline taxes, $328 in state income taxes, and $75 in other deductible taxes. What is his deduction for taxes?

Procedure

Operation	Keyboard Entry	Function Touch	Display	Description
Set decimal to zero places				
Clear registers and display		C	0	
Enter property taxes	740	+	740	
Enter sales taxes	115	+	855	Running total
Enter gasoline taxes	190	+	1045	Running total
Enter state income taxes	328	+	1373	Running total
Enter other deductible taxes	75	+	1448	Total

George Lincoln may deduct $1,448 for taxes paid.

ADDING SCHEDULE A

The calculator works very well as an adding machine. In this example, Mr. Williams has completed the part of his income tax preparation that is the most time consuming—that of itemizing all his deductions. Now, he must add up these deductions.

Adding Deductions

Alexander Williams has completed the entries he will make on his Schedule A. He has determined that his medical deductions amount to $412.40, his contribution deductions amount to $300.40, his tax expense deductions amount to $1812.99, his interest expense deductions amount to $1222.55, and his miscellaneous deductions amount to $340.00. What is the amount Mr. Williams should show as his itemized deductions?

Procedure

Operation	Keyboard Entry	Function Touch	Display	Description
Set decimal to two places				
Clear registers and display		C	0.00	
Enter medical deductions	412.40	+	412.40	
Enter contributions	300.40	+	712.80	Running total
Enter tax expense	1812.90	+	2525.79	Running total
Enter interest expense	1222.55	+	3748.34	Running total
Enter miscellaneous deductions	340.00	+	4048.74	Total

Mr. Williams will show $4048.74 as his itemized deductions.

TAXABLE INCOME

After all deductions and exemptions have been subtracted from gross income, we have what is known as **taxable income**. This is the amount upon which the tax rate is applied to determine the amount of tax.

Taxable Income Calculation

Ronald Noble has a gross income of $14,459, and deductions from gross income in the amount of $945. The amount of his personal exemptions is $2250, and his itemized deductions amount to $3854. What is his taxable income?

Procedure

Operation	Keyboard Entry	Function Touch	Display	Description
Set decimal to zero places				
Clear registers and display		C	0	
Enter gross income	14459	+	14459	Gross income
Enter deductions from gross income	945	−	13514	Adjusted gross income
Enter personal exemptions	2250	−	11264	
Enter itemized deductions	3854	−	7410	Taxable income

Mr. Noble's taxable income is $7410.

Index

Index

A

B

C

P

Q

R

S